Brava!

All proceeds from the sale of this book
go to providing bras for those in need.

Each of the writers in this book generously donated
their pieces to this publication and this cause.

Printed in the United States of America

First Edition

Library of Congress Cataloging-in-Publication Data

Brava Logo by Paul Miyamoto
Book Design by Pamela Fernuik Hodges

C O N T E N T S

GREETINGS by Daquetta Jones, former Executive Director, YWCA-GCR   10

HOW BRAVA! CAME TO BE by Marion Roach Smith   13

2015 page 15

2016 page 57

2017 page 99

2018 page 133

Brava!

BIOGRAPHIES of all the badass supportive writers   186

ACKNOWLEDGEMENTS thank you very much   197

2015
page 15

MY BOSUM BUDDY by Jillina Baxter   17

IMPLANTING DESIRE by Diane Cameron   20

BRA STORY by Alice Lichtenstein   23

THE ONE by Alifair Skebe   26

BREAST TRAINING by Patrice Malatestinic   29

SWIMMING AU NATUREL by Mary Scanlan   32

THESE BREASTS ARE MINE by Ruth Pelhan   35

THE NEIGHBRAHOOD by Jospeh Di Bari   39

NOW THAT'S A GIANT BRA by Melissa Frenyea   42

BOOBY TRAP by Tina Lincer   45

JUST THE BRA FOR THIS by Denise DiNoto   48

AMERICAN MARRIAGE by Marion Roach Smith   51

JOB DESCRIPTION by Megan Culhane Galbraith   53

2016

page 57

AN ODE TO MY FAVORITE by Katelynn Ulrich   59

MY LIFE IN BRAS by Megan Willis   62

LATE BLOOMER by Sarah Marquise   66

PROTECTING THE MILKING MACHINE by Sandra DiNoto   68

SOLILOQUY IN B FLAT by Brenda Kilianski   71

I AM NOT WEARING A BRA by Pamela Fernuik Hodges   74

RESTRICTIONS by Shavina Richardson   77

A DECADE BEFORE HER FIRST BRA by Kate Cohen   79

ENLISTING SUPPORT (& SOLDIERS) AT TARGET by Lisa Barone   82

MY TRIPLE "A" LIFE by Deirdre Greco   88

MY BRA by Opal Ingram   91

UNRULY UNDERWIRE by Denise DiNoto   92

THE SKIN OF MY TEETH by Sara Weeks   95

2017

page 99

MEMOIR OF BRAS PAST (BY A FLAT CHESTED WOMAN) by Susan Megna   101

THE TRAINING BRA by Alyssa Talanker   104

WHAT IS PRETTY by Denise DiNoto   106

MY BRA IS BLUE by Opal Ingram   109

UNDERWORLD by Carol Tyman   110

NO LONGER FRIENDS by Shavina Richardson   112

MY PLASTRON by Jennifer Hixon   114

TAGGING ALONG by Dan New   116

B...B...BRA by Sara Weeks   120

THAT ESSENTIAL GIRL by Diane Cameron   124

CHILDLESSNESS by Susan Comninos   127

DOWN TO THE WIRE by Tina Lincer   129

Brava!

2018

page 133

THE BIGGEST GAMBLE A WOMAN CAN TAKE by Christine McCue 135

JUST LIKE ALL THE OTHER GIRLS by Mary Scanlan 137

PLAYTEX 8267 by Denise DiNoto 140

THE BRA by Opal Ingram 143

SIS-BOOM-BRA by Tina Lincer 145

BACK IN THE DAY by Dan New 148

SOUTIEN by D. Colin 152

IMAGE OF SUPPORT by Jill Bryce 155

CONFESSIONS OF CORSETRY by Grace Pell 158

I AM YOUR BRA by Jamere Shelby 164

MY PLACE by Debra Townsend 166

BOOB WORLD by Sara Weeks 169

THEY - THEM - MINE by Leslie Sittner 173

TO STRAP OR NOT TO STRAP by Alyssa Talanker 176

MY GRANDMOTHER AT 50 by Nareen Luz Rivas 179

KILOMETER 41 by Pamela Fernuik Hodges 182

GREETINGS
by Daquetta Jones
former Executive Director,
YWCA-GCR

YWCA of the Greater Capital Region (YWCA-GCR) is dedicated to eliminating racism, empowering women and promoting peace, justice, freedom and dignity for all.

Since 1883, YWCA-GCR has served women in the City of Troy and Greater Capital Region areas. Today, YWCA-GCR is one of the area's largest providers of supportive housing to both single women and women with children who would otherwise be homeless or living in substandard housing.

In addition to homelessness prevention, economic empowerment, food security and other supportive services, every day, YWCA-GCR houses 104 women and over 50 children. YWCA-GCR is a local YWCA Association of YWCA USA. YWCA collective power serves over 2.3 million women, girls and their families in the United States. YWCA collective power reaches across 122 countries, serving 25 million women and girls annually!

With all of the resources, services and programs YWCA-

GCR provides, in 2014 we realized an essential item we were not providing; BRAS! It took a generous, giving and action-driven person to bring this to our attention and HELP us do something about it. That person is Marion Roach-Smith!

She brought all of her talents as a community activist, writer, author and educator, with other like-minded people, such as YWCA-GCR's former Director of Development and Marketing, Malissa Pilette-McClennon, to create BraVa! with YWCA of the Greater Capital Region women and girls in mind.

If not for Marion's decision to be cultivated by YWCA-GCR after being honored in 2014 as YWCA-GCR's 14th Annual Resourceful Women's Awards honoree, she and her husband's desire to support YWCA-GCR's Adopt-A-Family program, BraVa! may not have happened.

This philanthropic decision to support a family was the awakening moment -- that women, girls and nonbinary people need of BRAS!

Since 2014 we have raised over 3,000 brand new bras with tags and have distributed nearly 75% of all bras collected for FREE! In addition, 100% of the proceeds benefits YWCA-GCR!

In 2018, BraVa! expanded to Western NY in partnership with YWCA Western NY and Sheryl Duquette, who learned of BraVa! from interview with Marion and me on public radio with Susan Arbetter.

2019 will mark the 5th Annual BraVa! event in partnership with The Arts Center of the Capital Region, on Friday, November 8, at The Arts Center. YWCA-GCR is about supporting and advancing the empowerment of women and girls. When you're out shopping for a bra, think of YWCA-GCR and purchase a bra for them! We need you to continue filling this essential need.

When you go out to purchase a new bra, please consider buying a second one to donate to YWCA-GCR. Monetary contributions toward the purchase of bras can be made online at www.ywca-gcr.org/donation or you can drop off or mail bras year round to YWCA-GCR at 21 First Street, Troy, NY 12180.

For more information on how you can support YWCA-GCR, please contact us at info@ywca-gcr.org or call 518-274-7100.

A special thank you to all of our supporters, logo designers, contributing artists and sponsors that help make BraVa! possible.

On behalf of YWCA of the Greater Capital Region, our team, board and those that benefit, thank you! ΔΔ

With gratitude,
Daquetta Jones,
former Executive Director

HOW BRAVA! CAME TO BE
By Marion Roach Smith

The request came in December, 2014: Please purchase holiday gifts for a woman and her three children, all residents of the YWCA of the Greater Capital Region (YWCA-GCR). First on the holiday wish list was a bra for the mother, followed by her simple statement, "I don't have any."

Suddenly a compelling story revealed itself in this small detail. The mother must have left in the middle of the night, probably in her pajamas, taking her three children and little else. Maybe it was domestic violence that drove her from her home, but whatever the cause, she left without a bra, meaning that today she can't go out and find work, go to the pharmacy, or shop for food. In short, she cannot start over.

I could not tell and I knew I should not ask for any specifics, but I did call a contact at the YWCA-GCR and ask if I had it right – the basics of the story and its meaning. Yes, I was told, and that the need for bras was great and difficult to meet. Those who arrive at the YWCA-GCR in need are every shape and size, after all, and many of them lack basic clothing, including bras.

"I'm going to go get you some," I think I said, hanging up the phone without a clue how to do so.

And so, BraVa! was born.

BraVa! is a night of memoir about the place of bras in our lives. Each year, on one night in early November, writers read, recite and sing as the audience listens, laughs and cries along with them, and each year we raise bras, our awareness and our spirits. The price of admission to BraVa! includes bringing a brand new bra to the event.

Our first BraVa!, held in 2015, was standing room only. And we've filled the theater every year since. I've never heard the same story twice. We've heard from people across all lines of diversity, and every year we learn more about the power of the bra to get us out the door to live our lives. To date, we've raised 3,000 bras for people in need, and have expanded the program to make these bras available to anyone in our community or beyond.

In this, our fifth year, we celebrate the bra with this book and with the knowledge that if you give a bra, you give someone the support needed to get out and start again. ΔΔ

Marion Roach Smith,
38 Double D, a firm supporter of BraVa!

Our first BraVa! took place in 2015.
It was a sold-out night.
Here is what the audience heard.
Before each piece are the words
of our emcees for the night.

Brava!

The bra has a diverse, controversial, and yet common history,
both in the world and on our bodies. Here to bring us one version
of that history is Jillina Baxter.

MY BOSOM BUDDY
by Jillina Baxter

I know some people who aren't comfortable

with their body image

It's a one on one battle that becomes an all-out scrimmage

Some days I feel like I'm just hanging on by a strap

I need someone to intercede to stand in the gap

At the age of 15 is when I started training

I wasn't considered a knockout,

but consciousness slowly regaining

This flower child was considered a late bloomer

By the time I was 28 I discovered Victoria's Secret

and put and end to that rumor

I didn't find it funny or side-splitting

But I eventually adjusted like a bra fitting

Brava!

Body insured as in full coverage

Some women come with baggage,

but should continue to carry on like luggage

Well known in some circles as in semi

I have so much more to offer than Demi

It lifted me up when others let me down

I wore a strapless one underneath my evening gown

Some are made fashion and others for sports

Pairing with panties or matching boy shorts

So I dove in head first and took the plunge

I cleaned up good just like a sponge

I've never been to Bali visited Raleigh

But like L.L. Cool J I'm Going Back to Cali

Haunted by unwanted attention

Sometimes the girls are fighting with each other

like they need an intervention

Tried to push up on me, but pulled a fast one

Won't be the first and sure won't be the last one

A measure of a woman should not be based

on her bust size

But for what beats within her chest

and this is the reason

I don't trust guys

Some bras are designed for nursing

But sometimes the way they fit

I will refrain from cursing

Hated the feeling when my boobs became engorged

But went ahead and like a signature I forged

Well in all fairness I stood in front of the mirror

examining my own bareness

I'm not some charity case,

raised money for Breast Cancer Awareness

I realized I don't need a boob job

to build up my self-esteem

I thank God for making me the way I am

without a stitch or a seam

Those painful memories rubbed me the wrong way

like wearing an underwire

Ended abruptly like the last episode

of Grace Under Fire

I've learned the hard way,

but I continue to study

Thanks for your support,

my bosom buddy ΔΔ

*Do we ever really love our bras? If so, learning to love them
is a process that begins with learning how you feel about your body.
Diane Cameron has some thoughts on that in her piece,
Implanting Desire.*

IMPLANTING DESIRE

By Diane Cameron

A few weeks ago I called my friend Miriam to ask what
my godchild, Rita, would like for her tenth birthday. I
do believe that it is the special prerogative of godpar-
ents to buy gifts that the parents won't spring for. In
past years this meant I bought a tape player, a drum set
and even skating lessons.

So when I asked Miriam what Rita was hoping for,
her mom said, "Well, she's asking for breast implants."
We laughed. But I was haunted by Rita's wish. At nine
years old, this smart, funny and athletic little girl needed
breasts and she thought she had to buy them? I was
undone.

Now, a few years back when she wanted her ears
pierced at age 7, I knew I could not take her to get ears
pierced, but I could give her an assortment of shiny,

stick-on earrings to met her girlish need to be sparkly and bejeweled. But what need could I possibly try to meet for a ten-year-old who wants breast implants?

It wasn't the wanting breasts that rocked me. I remember wanting them too. Well, what I really wanted was to wear a bra. I was older — 12 or 13 — but I had no need for a bra. The cotton tank tops with the pink rosette trim worked fine until I was at least 18. (Well, OK, maybe 28). So I understood. I was the last girl at Latimer Junior High to get a bra and I only wore it on gym days when my mother finally understood that I had social needs in the girl's locker room and not for any physiological reason.

But still, Rita's wish threw me.

I work in marketing and I studied communication theory and even with that I know how easily I can be persuaded by advertising to suddenly "need" something (Eileen Fisher shoes, a merlot sweater, a convertible bra) — things that I didn't even know existed yesterday. My "Huh, that's interesting" gets converted to "Other women probably all have one of these" and then finally to, "I need that."

One of the big issues with advertising (and now the way that it slippy-slides into our social media) is that it encourages us to have relationships with things and to believe that products can be trusted when people can't.

So it makes sense that Rita, who wants breasts, is seeking a product solution. Rather than resort to praying for breasts and bras like her mother and I did at 12, Rita's expectation is that she can buy breasts. It would be funny if it weren't so frightening.

So what did I give Rita? I decided to go with clothes and books and music. But I also bought her a diary, the kind with a lock and key. I wanted to pass along the satisfaction of writing down thoughts and feelings, and even disappointments and unrequited love — to give her that important tool for her girlhood repertoire.

What I most wish for Rita, this bright and shiny ten year-old, is that she will survive with her psyche intact. I'm hoping that the adults in her life — all of us — will teach her to find what she needs in her self — and not off the shelf — and that we will remember to see her as more than another bright star in the consumer constellation. ΔΔ

Brava!

Adolescence is hell on bras and bras are hell on adolescence.
Every woman has a story about that,
including Alice Lichtenstein.

BRA STORY

by Alice Lichtenstein

I tell my writing students to write what scares them, and I think I have provided them with a good model, having written three novels on topics that certainly scared me, but it isn't until I hear an announcement on the radio, calling for essay submissions on the topic of bras, that I say to myself, I can't do that. I absolutely cannot face that time in my life.

I was a tomboy. No, I did not want to be a boy; I did not want a boy's psyche (I thought boys were fairly stupid). I wanted to run, throw, climb, wrestle. I wanted a boy's freedom to move and to express myself. And I had it. Until one afternoon when the fifth grade girls were separated from the fifth grade boys, denied recess (the first ominous sign), to attend an assembly on the onslaught of physical changes soon to befall us. Blood, hair, breasts. The three plagues. I left that room terrified and angry and vowing that I wasn't going to succumb.

The breasts began as breasts do—soft, fairly innocuous bumps. I had a solution. Tight T-shirts filched from my younger sister's dresser drawer, worn under baggy sweatshirts, under baggy sweaters. I adopted a nightly regime of knuckling my breasts with both fists, hoping to flatten them. For a while this seemed to work. And then it didn't. That summer at riding camp, an older, cooler girl asks me, the wonder and admiration clear in her voice, "How does it feel to ride without a bra?" I am stunned and cannot answer. She can tell.

Bra. At the age of twelve, I cannot say the word without experiencing a wave of nausea. Still, I understand where things are at now. I have to buy one.

When I return home from camp, I break open my piggy bank; I steal some change from the dish on the top of my father's bureau. I am not going to tell my mother that I need a bra. I am not going to admit to the world that I have breasts. The truth is, I have never seen a woman's breasts other than those in the pages of my older brother's Playboy, and those, he informs me, are fake. Real breasts, he says, are hairy like a gorilla's. He knows, he says, because he's seen them. I do not answer. My own breasts, thank God, are smooth. They do not have hairs. Yet.

I fill my marbles pouch with coins and take the bus to the shopping center where there is one department store. I buy a bra without even trying it on. I have no idea what the letters mean or the numbers. It is white; it is small. I have enough money to pay for it. At home, I shove it to the back of my sock drawer. I am filled with unaccountable shame. I have a desperate secret that I cannot reveal to anyone — least of all to myself — I am a woman.

A few weeks later, I try on the bra. The mirror is on the back of the bathroom door. The house, I have made sure, is empty. No one has taught me how to put on a bra. I hang the straps over my shoulders, the back ends flapping like an unstrung harness. A harness. That's how the thing feels. It's tight. It restrains me. I take a deep breath and pull on my blouse, bringing the edges of the fabric together, buttoning the buttons with trembling fingers. Oh my God. There's the shelf. The shelf that all grown women seem to have, a slope that juts from the sternum, dropping off into nothingness above the solar plexus. I never quite understood before how the shelf formed; I hypothesized that breasts eventually grew to one large loaf. No. The bra creates the shelf. I have one.

A few years later, women are burning their bras, reclaiming their freedom. I join them in spirit if not in action. I have come to see that my disgust at wearing a bra sprang from a gut-wrenching fear of losing my girl-self, my confidence and my freedom. Forty years later, I am the mother of two daughters, whom I very consciously raised to celebrate their bodies and themselves. These daughters couldn't wait to buy bras. We bought them together, then we went for a long run. ΔΔ

Brava!

You know when it's the one, that bra that does for you what you need it to do. Alifair Skebe learned what support can truly be when she met her first good bra, as reported in The One.

THE ONE
by Alifair Skebe

I place the cereal box from my basket on a shelf and pull the other boxes into line. I've been re-shelving the store for two hours. MacFrugal's, where I work, is a closeout store filled with misfit products. Behind the stack, a figurine of Ernie from Sesame Street is pushed all the way back and tipped over. Ernie's shirt is scuffed, and his smile rubbed out. Dirt lines the cracks in his knees. I slip him into my apron pocket

Today, I'm done at five, although it feels much later. Sixty pages of PoliSci and an Econ paper to do tonight. I glance at my watch – 4:58. I push the cart into motion, and the wheels click and veer to the right. I stop short at the time clock. Add four hours to the weekly paycheck at $5.25 an hour. I've got to get new tires on the Volvo. As I'm standing there, my right bra strap snaps and I'm left hanging.

In my eighteen years of life until this moment, I can honestly say that I hate bra shopping and I hate bras, which I hate only second to my big, lumpy breasts. I've resewn my old, white cotton "over-the-shoulder-boulder-holders" countless times since I was thirteen. Lucky for me, a new shipment of bras between $3 and $4 arrived today. This will be my first bra purchase, and I think I can just afford it.

In women's wear, I wade my fingers through the circular rack of bras over satin, silk, and lace. It's like the bras are singing to me, and I'm captivated, drawn closer by an invisible force. I grab a red lace bra with black ribbing, then a purple floral, a satin beige for modesty, a black cotton for utility, about ten others, and finally a dark blue lace bra.

I take my horde to the dressing room, step inside, and pull the door tightly behind us. The whole room is the size of a port-a-potty and about as sturdy. Fluorescent lights tint my skin blue-green. The walls are so thin, I can hear shuffling outside the door. I wiggle out of my shirt. Then I shimmy into the bra straps. No mirror to see myself in this weird bra dance.

Suddenly, I'm thirteen in Dillard's department store dressing room, and my mom is saying, "No, Carolyn, you're not a C cup. You don't need to go up a cup size. You're bigger around the chest. A 36B. I'm a B cup and you certainly can't be bigger than that." A saleswoman peeks her head in. "Need any help, ladies?" Mom shoos her away. We're only here because my boobs hurt in gym class when I have to run around the track and in dance class during jumping drills. In fact, if I had those nice, pert breasts Stacy has, I wouldn't be here fumbling through the bra section.

"But it doesn't feel right," I whine, "It feels too loose." I look down to see a clear inch between my breasts, and the bra is stretched across them like a thin rope bridge across a canyon.

"Bras aren't meant to be comfortable," she says.

To make matters worse, when I'm really exercising with my new bra on, my boobs pop out of the bottom and I have to get them back inside before anyone notices. I hold my chest when I run, and soon I stop running altogether. "A 12-minute mile, Carolyn. You came in last again." Oh well, Ms. Thwaite, I guess I'm not a runner. A few months later, I quit dance. Sorry, Ms. Cotton, I guess I'm not a dancer.

I find myself in a three-by-three dressing room with fifteen bras scattered at my feet. Reaching around my back, I snap the eyelets into place. Periwinkle flowers and dots in the lace pattern brighten against my white skin. The underwire cradles my breasts and I feel supported, even slightly uplifted. I twist a little. The bra gives, but stays in place, resisting my movements. I look down – the bra secures the gap between my breasts. This is the one.

I re-dress and put each bra back on its hanger. Outside, a mother and daughter examine the training bras. The girl smiles at the bra in my hand. I return the smile, blush, and hand her Ernie from my pocket.

At the register, I slip the bra to my co-worker Annie. She blurts out, "Oh sexy! I bet your boyfriend's gonna like this one." Customers from the next aisle careen their heads to gawk at my purchase.

I smile back at Annie and reply, "Yeah, I bet I'm gonna like this one." ΔΔ

Hold a bra up to the light and see it in a new way.
It can take it. Here's how Patrice Malatestinic
tells its tale in Breast Training.

BREAST TRAINING
by Patrice Malatestinic

Descended from pear shaped nymphs,

Small breasted, big hearted,

I hold endomorphic attitudes.

Regarding Brassieres: Why bother?

Undershirted and cotton camisoled girls

covet maturation.

Training bras keep budding breasts

and nipples under wraps

Bridging the gap to AAA status

(like big league baseball).

29

Brava!

Jane Russell, Miss Monroe, Dolly: Watch Out!

In 5th grade, bras lift and

Separate the men from the boys.

Maid form and Wonderbra follow function.

Points become curves, and, if not melons, implants.

Once, women, weak and breathless,

corseted into place, by

Paste stiffened linen and steel stays,

Watched boys rail playing at hardball and war.

The 1917 US War Industries Board banned corsets

To free up metal for WWI.

(28 tons gleaned)

Inadvertently freeing women for revolution.

1968 Atlantic City hosts Miss America.

The boardwalk's Freedom Trash Can

Brava!

Fills with stilettos, eyelashes, bras and Playboy;

One match could transform

oppression to billowing plumes.

Today's evolving sexuality

Begins in the crib,

Babies in bikinis,

Bratz bras in pre-K.

Bras as lingerie or sportswear,

provocative frosting or female athletic supporters,

Miss the point: Breasts have a job.

Ask any newborn hogging the prizes ornamented

within Victoria's Secret. ∆∆

Brava!

What we think and how we think about our bras and ourselves,
changes over time, with some definitive milestones
along the way, some more vivid than others, but few
as vivid as the case of Mary Scanlan's falsies.

SWIMMING AU NATUREL

by Mary Scanlan

It was the early sixties. I was entering my junior year in college and my brother Jim was entering his senior year in a prep seminary. We were travelling together to Miami from New York to celebrate winter break. Our parents had moved to Coral Gables in Florida where my Dad had started a new job. Jim and I were excited about spending a week in warmth and relaxation there, away from school.

The day after we arrived, we walked from our parents' home for a swim at the nearby Venetian Pool. Now on the list of the National Register of Historic Places, it's a public swimming pool in Coral Gables, completed in 1924. Created from an old coral rock quarry, it is a beautiful Mediterranean Revival pool, with coral surrounding the water, a Venetian style bridge, and lots of Spanish architecture. Fresh water is recycled into the pool every day with natural ground filtration. This was not at all what we had known as a public pool in the New York City area.

Delighted, my brother and I entered through the complex,

amazed at full size palm trees adorning the property, and a grotto where caves stretch back over twelve feet into the hill-side across the pool. We found a spot to settle on the sandy sunning area. It was all so tranquil and luxurious. We were in a world where nature and antiquity came together.

We decided to race each other after our initial dip and start-ed doing an Australian crawl together. Jim was over six feet tall, muscular and fit, much bigger and stronger than I, and a good swimmer to boot. I, at that time in my life, was strong, but thin and not the greatest swimmer. Convincing myself that I would be more attractive and desirable with a bit of chest, I had purchased a new bathing suit and a set of falsies to enhance my very flat chest. These were to be inserted in the breast cups of the new suit.

On the second lap of our crawl I was suddenly aware that one of my falsies, those adorable vanilla white foam rubber cups, was floating on the pure water in front of me. Horrified, I stage-whispered to Jim, "Go get that. It's mine!" Equally hor-rified, he whispered back to me, "I'm not touching that thing." All of his seminary training about sexuality swam to his head. The calm day became a tsunami for me when another bather saw the falsie. Holding it above his head, he twisted the foam rubber cup around, looked at it quizzically, and then placed it gently on the top of the coral rock at the edge of the pool.

And there it remained, foam rubber in the midst of natu-ral rock and fresh water, on display for all to ponder as they enjoyed nature's bounty in the largest freshwater pool in the country. Swimmers went by and said, "What's that? Looks like something very archaic." And then they swam away, leaving the foam rubber for another day in the sun.

My brother and I left early that first afternoon. The specter of the falsie overshadowed our day. Jim was furious with me for embarrassing him. I was furious with me for letting the slip happen, and upset with him for not rescuing me. We said nothing to our parents, but growled at each other at night when we recalled the scene. We returned to the pool the next day and the next and the next. During that week, no one touched or moved the falsie. It had become part of nature's beauty.

Unable to stand it any longer, I finally swam, underwater, over to the rock on our last day of vacation, furtively looked around and removed the unnatural object from its pristine post, when I thought no one else was looking, except my brother, of course.

We left the Venetian Pool, never to return. And, I never returned to wearing falsies, bearing up under the strain of being flat chested until I gave birth to our children. Even then, I was jeered by nurses in the hospital where our first child was born for being small chested and probably unable to nurse a baby. Thirteen months later I stopped nursing our daughter and was never flat chested again. ΔΔ

Pride, shame, pride, shame. One day a woman decides that enough is enough, and if she's Ruth Pelham, she puts that moment to music and calls it, These Breasts Are Mine.

THESE BREASTS ARE MINE
by Ruth Pelham

Oh my breasts hang down
And when I'm running through my town
How they bounce, how they bob
How they jiggle all around
But I'd never trade my big breasts in
I like my breasts just fine
'Cause these breasts are mine

When I was an adolescent
And my breasts began to grow
I developed quite a complex
I thought "Big breasts! No, no, no!"

Brava!

Now I'd never trade my big breasts in
I like my breasts just fine
'Cause these breasts are mine

I've had endless conversations
With myself about my breasts
Voices saying, "They're so ugly, heavy
Beautiful, the best"
Still, I'd never trade my big breasts in
I like my breasts just fine
'Cause these breasts are mine

There are breasts so very different
Round and small and very firm
Breasts like those are surely beautiful
But for them no, I don't yearn
No I'd never trade my big breasts in
I like my breasts just fine
'Cause these breasts are mine
In these times I know the chances

I could have one breast, not two
And if ever that did happen
Then I hope here's what I'd do
I'd sing, I'd never trade my one breast in
I like my breast just fine
'Cause this breast is mine

And I know the time could come
When I could have no breasts at all
I would say goodbye to both my breasts
And stand up proud and tall
I'd sing, I'd never trade my own chest in
I like my chest just fine
'Cause this chest is mine
Breast implants and other dangers
Make me angry with disgust
Liposuction, crazy diets
Doctors getting rich on us
Hell, I'd never trade my big breasts in
I like my breasts just fine

'Cause these breast are mine
In these years I've gotten smarter
Gotten louder, gotten wise
I'm not hooked by advertisers
Selling products, selling lies
No, I'd never trade my big breasts in
I like my breasts just fine
'Cause these breasts are mine

Women all around the world
Are building pride and dignity
We're standing up for every sister
Building strength in unity
No, we'd never trade our own breasts in
We like our breasts just fine
'Cause these breasts are mine." ∆∆

Brava!

And what about the beholder of the bra? What is he or she to think of this contraption? Joseph DiBari got more than an eyeful when he took in his first bra. He turned the experience into a piece called The Neighbrahood.

THE NEIGHBRAHOOD

By Joseph Di Bari

Even as a young boy the huge cups swinging on the clothesline fascinated me. Miss Greenberg was the nicest lady on the block. Zaftig and kind, hers was the best door to knock on for Halloween.

My Dad said to me in private, "She reminds me of a '57 Cadillac."

I thought her a jolly, friendly and kind woman not worthy of the brunt of a joke. The bra went out like clockwork at 2 pm each day. You could set your watch by it.

It was not a well-to-do neighborhood so I imagined that she only had the two bras, which she alternated between washings. We were all poor but no one was dirty. All of our clothes were worn and faded but the bra was always gleaming evidence of the care given by personal attention. No machine-washing for this vital accoutrement.

It was a metaphor for life, something of value that served an important purpose but had the mystique that would grab and hold on to a young boy's attention. I fantasized about the day I would somehow be given permission to see one close up. I shaded my eyes and carefully observed the enigma, the frilly lace top and double clip in the back. The dangling straps that made me think of my fingers making the OK sign. I studied and strategized the garment devising the most efficient way to unhook and peel away my gift-wrap to reveal the elusive and mysterious Bonnie and Clyde.

The bra gave me hope. It taught me if I worked hard enough and was good I would be rewarded. It was my beacon shining my way through puberty into manhood. The dependable symbol that illustrated if you cared for something it will remain as beautiful as the first day you ever saw it.

It was very windy that Friday, and there was no bra on the line. I wondered if Miss Greenberg was ill. I looked down from my second story widow and saw the bra on the ground tumbling in the breeze to rest near a puddle of mud. I dashed down the stairs only to see the teenagers playing with it, using it as a slingshot and mimicking old ladies donning it as a babushka. They ripped it apart. They had no idea of its importance, its reverence. The bra was torn to shreds.

I went and gathered the pieces and had no idea what should be done. If I returned it, it may seem like I was the l'il perv downstairs. I threw it in the garbage pale, but before I put the lid on closing its fate, it spoke to me. The tiny label said 44 C underwire Chantel 3281. I ripped it off. I knew I couldn't remember all of that. I ran upstairs and smashed my piggy bank. I counted $23.89 in change. Would that be enough? I took the tag and a jingly paper bag full of my booty to the Mason lingerie store on the corner of Pure and Benevolent. I concocted a story that it was my Mom's birthday and she saw the bra in a magazine. The big question, how much will one cost?

"Well Sir", the young lady said, "this bra is thirty-five dollars plus tax".

My heart sunk.

"How much do you have?"

"23.89," I sheepishly admitted.

"You are quite lucky sir, we are having a sale just for this one day and the price with tax is 23.79. That gives you a dime for bubble gum. Would you like it gift-wrapped sir?"

"Yes Ma'am." I liked being called sir.

I got my gum and snuck back into the house to see Miss Greenberg staring blankly out the window at the empty clothes-line. It was her turn for trick-or-treat. I left the pretty pink box at her door, rang her bell and ran away. The next afternoon at 2pm a brand new Chantel 3281 swung in the breeze. ∆∆

*How do I love thee? Let me count the ways, and please let me
include on that list your bra. When someone feels this way
about your bra, you are one lucky woman, or so it seems in the
relationship between Missy Frenyea and her partner.
The piece is called, simply, Now That's a Giant Bra!*

Now That's a Giant Bra!
By Melissa Frenyea

When I first spotted my partner, Lori, with her long dark hair,
hour-glass figure, and considerable double D bosom, I thought
Wonder Woman herself had walked into the room. Little did I
know from that first glimpse of her Amazonian rack what lies
beneath…

Behind every ample bosom, there is an ample bra. During my
first intimate encounter with Lori, I learned this very quickly. No
bra I had ever wrangled with was like hers with its intimidating
rows of shark's teeth fasteners. My own AA bras have only two
fasteners and honestly one is probably enough. Needless to say,
I was rather ham fisted pressing and pulling while attempting to
pop the hood of this mysterious brassiere. I finally surrendered
and asked for help. Clearly, I needed to re-watch those Happy
Days scenes in which Fonzi demonstrates bra removal tech-
niques using Potsy's mother's bra wrapped around a radiator.

As Lori and I began to spend more time together, I became
more skilled with and grew more fascinated by the bras of the

full-figured woman. Did you know it's not atypical for some women to wear two bras during exercise? It's true. Lori explained the reason was to battle the appearance of "Uniboob." Uniboob is a phenomenon caused by squishing two large boobs together and attempting to control the twain with a compression-style sports bra. This creates one giant breast—aka "Uniboob"—which bounces dangerously as a single being during exercise. To reduce the appearance of Uniboob, Lori, and others like her, resort to using a regular bra to lift and separate and a compression bra over the top to keep things under control. Understandably, this is not comfortable for any period of time exceeding three minutes or for any high-impact activity like jogging or hiking or running with bulls. As an avid hiker, I shuddered at the thought of having to wear two bras at a time. My laundry hamper would be full of bras within a few days. Surely there was a better solution.

After two years of dating, Lori and I moved in together. Since we were sharing a home, I made an executive decision that it was now acceptable to purchase each other underwear. I was determined to find her a sports bra targeted for the full-figured woman. My quest introduced me to a new and fascinating subculture. I read countless reviews online from women with dimensions in the key of DD, EE, GG (and beyond!) singing the praises of a special breed of bras that enabled them to comfortably exercise without the horror of Uniboob. Their thoughtful reflections helped me narrow down my choice. In the end, I chose a product called the Shock Absorber D+ Max Support based on a reviewer who tested the strength of the bra by using it as a hammock for her Yorkshire Terrier. Her recommendation stated, "If this bra can hold my eight pound dog and she feels safe, just think how my breasts feel." I ordered three.

When the box arrived, I ripped it open with a curious B-cup friend present. What I held in my hands made us both gasp. Never before had we seen such a contraption. It was not so much a bra as it was an engineering marvel. The reinforced, double-padded, triple-wide-zero-back-fat straps, the shock resistant clasps, the intricate stitchery… staggering. This was the Hoover Dam of the Bra World. The ghost of Jane Russell in moisture-wicking fabric form. There was a moment of reverent silence and then my friend whispered, "Now that's a giant bra."

Turns out the Shock Absorber D+ was a perfect fit and opened up a whole new world of outdoor enjoyment for me and my full-figured gal. Since that package arrived, Lori and I and those giant bras have logged countless hours and hundreds of miles together on the Appalachian Trail hiking up and over the hills of New York and New England. As we walk along in the woods planning for our future, I continue to steal glances at that super-hero bosom. And now I know what lies beneath — a remarkable bra worthy of my Wonder Woman. △△

Brava!

*On? Off? On again, off again? In her piece, Booby Trap,
Tina Lincer tackles the question of to wear or go bare.*

BOOBY TRAP
by Tina Lincer

At 16, I took off my bra. It was 1971. Woodstock may have happened without me, but the Age of Aquarius still exerted its energy and glorious sense of freedom. There was nothing more liberating to a moody, restless teenage girl than going braless.

It was the thrill of flouting convention, of challenging the status quo and protocols that had a tendency to hold girls back. Or at least it felt that way at a time when girls politely sewed aprons and baked popovers in home economics while boys in shop classes got to assert their power by hacking through hardwood with a table saw.

Braless, I could carve out my own identity and style.

Besides feeling good, it was a way to align with something important. I'm not sure the words feminist, women's lib or bra-burner entered my thinking, but a wave of change in female roles was sweeping society, and the lowly bra emerged as a provocative, political symbol. It lifted and separated me from my mother, who graduated college at 19 and became a lifelong stay-at-home mom, something I found puzzling and disappointing.

No bra, no restrictions. If our underclothing were less confining, perhaps our lives would be so, too. I draped myself in bellbottoms and work boots, headbands and bandannas, work shirts and gauzy Mexican peasant tops.

But no bra.

Not that I needed one. I hadn't, truthfully, seen much growth in that region of my body since purchasing my first training bra at 12, a bad shopping experience made unnecessarily worse when my mother insisted I show the saleswoman how it fit. I hated both of them, my clueless mom and the squinty-eyed May's Department Store underwear lady who pried me from the dressing room. Puberty in public – could anything be more anguishing?

I was a skinny girl, barely 100 pounds. Who needed a bra?

Be free. Go unfettered. Don't be hung up.

My parents weren't exactly supportive. Not ones for frank talk, they spoke little, though their averted eyes said lots. I'm sure they were horrified, but maybe they decided to pick their battles. A battle of their teenage daughter's breasts didn't top their list.

At school, some girlfriends also decided to shed the straps, hooks and cotton cups that bound them. Thinking back, I pity those young male teachers at Cardozo High, the misters Conrad, Freda and Keck, teaching algebra, English and earth science, trying to fix their eyes on chairs instead of chests.

I abandoned my bra throughout college and afterward, as a young newspaper reporter in my first grown-up job. In good weather, I routinely rode my three-speed bike through city streets at night. Braless and fearless, I'd cycle down Central Avenue without a thought, my bouncy boobs feeling as light as my fast-pedaling feet.

Briefly, I lived in a co-ed house where no one owned a bra. To make extra cash, I occasionally modeled nude for a male photographer who was recommended by an artist friend. It was no big deal, really. No bra meant fewer impediments, and therefore anxieties, to disrobing.

(I'm both impressed and aghast at this now; the photographer could have been a sociopath or murderer, or both.)

Only once did I regret not draping myself in Maidenform like most other women. I'd boarded a crowded train in the Bronx. Crowded, that is, until everyone exited at one stop and I found myself the lone passenger on the Manhattan-bound train. A single man walked on, scanned the empty car, and sat — to my distress — right beside me. I endured the rest of ride staring at the ground, my folded arms squeezed across my cotton tee.

I went braless for seven years, until, at 23, I began planning my wedding, and a lacy bra entered the bridal couture. In the final moments — down to the wire, you could say — I succumbed.

At last, my bra went back on. Before long, I became enamored with styles of the day. Strapless and sports bras, bandeaus and bustiers, cushioned cups and push-ups filled my dresser drawers. A Victoria's Secret credit card slipped seamlessly into my wallet.

But I love thinking about the unrestricted braless years. These days, the first thing I do after getting home from work is change from my sweaters and skirts into jeans and a sweatshirt. Often, my bra takes a break, too. It's freeing, at any age. ΔΔ

Braval

Can we talk about bras and not talk about sex?
Perhaps we cannot. In her story, Just the Bra for This,
Denise DiNoto tackles just that.

JUST THE BRA FOR THIS
by Denise DiNoto

My older sisters and cousins laugh when they explain how they all knew it was time for them to start wearing a bra. When "the aunts" (my mom and her sisters) gave them hugs and rubbed their backs, surreptitiously checking for the presence of an elastic band, it meant you should be measuring yourself for band and cup size. I don't remember those hugs. Probably because I can barely remember a time when I didn't need to wear a bra.

Like most females in my family, I was an early bloomer and began wearing a bra before other girls my age. I come from a line of well-endowed women. I always knew I would be "blessed" in much the same fashion.

Bras were just a necessity. A piece of elastic designed to keep things in place. A required article of clothing which I couldn't wait to remove at the end of the day.

Things changed when I left college. I started dating and realized I was quite literally sitting under a gold mine. These breasts, which were so inconvenient given my narrow shoulders, were a way to attract attention from men.

Men love cleavage. I am fairly certain there are some scientific studies to support that claim. With the right bra, I have great cleavage, as I have been told by multiple men — and some women. My cleavage is a wonderful asset. Men notice it. Small chested women envy it. Once I realized cleavage was a source of power, I recognized the importance of equipping myself with proper tools to achieve the desired effect. Enter the padded push up bra.

Some might think a woman with a size 38D bust might not require a padded push up. Some might be mistaken. Without padding, my bosoms are big and bulbous, but not worthy of more than a glance.

Add the padding and push them up and my cleavage takes shape. Given the right v-neck shirt or dress, men notice my ample breasts instead of my wheelchair.

Oh, who am I kidding? People always notice the chair first. It's shiny, red and permanently attached to my butt. However, the right bra makes it easier for men to view me as a sexual being.

If you think women who use wheelchairs aren't sexual, you're wrong. We crave intimacy and connection as much as our non-disabled peers. We have sex and we like it!

Now, I view my bras as more than a requirement. They are essential accessories which play an important role in my daily fashion. Each day my bras are called upon to complete a vital task. My bras offer support and shape to my torso, and provide a boost of confidence which I imagine ambulatory women find in a killer pair of shoes.

I treat my bras with the respect they deserve. I clasp the band together before placing them in the wash. My bras are hung on my clothes rack to dry and never go in the dryer. Clothes dryers are mortal enemies to maintaining proper fit and shape. Nothing ruins underwire faster.

No longer do I limit myself to boring white. I wrap myself in color — red, pink, blue, magenta, peach and black. I have special occasion bras which I save for particular dresses or blouses. I can't wear just any old bra with my little black dress. I have to wear the padded orange and black push up with the air pillow inserts; the one which makes my uneven breasts look the same size. If I wear the fuschia gown, I need the minimizer which squashes in the back fat and gives me a smoother finish.

When I was temporarily living with my sister and her family, my nephew once asked, "Mom, how come Aunt Denise's bras are colorful and yours are only white?" My sister's former husband agreed that was a fantastic question. I was no longer allowed to hang my bras in the bathroom to dry.

A few years ago I made the mistake of buying a youth large shirt instead of an adult size. I tried it on, realizing my blunder as soon as I attempted to pull it down. The friend who was assisting me expressed concern, fearing I would not be able to wear the top — a killer red shirt with the word "Naughty" spelled in silver sparkles across the chest.

"Don't worry," I said calmly. "I have just the bra for this." ΔΔ

And what about the role of the bra in a long-term marriage?
How do you keep the love alive?
Let's ask Marion Roach Smith.

AMERICAN MARRIAGE
by Marion Roach Smith

I've just passed my 26th wedding anniversary and it's got me thinking about what's really important if you want to go the distance in marriage.

It's the small stuff, I think, like a moment I had recently with my husband. There we were, having a perfectly lovely drive in the country, zipping along, talking, a rare time alone. No one was over-caffeinated, everyone was sober.

I mean I'd like to blame it on the caffeine — but I can't — and I don't drink, so it's not that influence that propelled me to say what I did when yet another car zipped by with one of those oval stickers on the bumper portraying merely a number.

Have you wondered what they mean? I have. Those little oval stickers used to mean only that someone had touristed in some European city, perhaps even purchased there the vehicle they are now driving and proudly want to display that. Then those little oval stick-ons started to mean more (or less) than that, and I got confused.

The sticker on the car next to us read "70.3." Nothing more.

And as it whizzed into view I gave no time to the fairly sane man whose job in life it has become to put his index finger in the back of the neckline of my shirt and reel me in. Instead, before I asked what the sticker could possibly mean, I merely stuck my head out the window and yelled, "38 Double D!"

You know that feeling? Like you've passed a clot, or dodged a bullet, or otherwise just cleared the air of something you've long wanted to do? Maybe cats feel this way after the hurling of a hairball. I hope so. It felt good. Real good.

My husband was silent for a moment; the look on his face the one he gets when he is forced to quickly shove together the evidence before him into some narrative he can live with. He looked at the bumper sticker. He looked at me. And then he began to laugh in that way I have come to value as the ultimate paycheck of my life. If marriage is the hardest room to work in Vegas — and it is — at that moment all the slots were pouring out in my bucket as he laughed and laughed and laughed.

When he was finally able again to speak, he asked calmly, "You don't know what those stickers are, do you?"

"Nope."

"Triathalons. Iron Man competitions. Those represent the distances the people have gone."

"Huh."

Now I know. ΔΔ

Brava!

So a bra walks into a job interview, after answering an ad that reads like this -- if it's written by Megan Culhane Galbraith.

JOB DESCRIPTION
by Megan Culhane Galbraith

Job title: Executive Director of Support Systems

Reports to: Vice President of Infrastructure & Engineering

Job Description

The Executive Director of Support Systems is a senior level appointee who works at the intersection of support and indecency. This position provides full-time care, protection, and counsel to two clients, The Girls, throughout puberty, young adulthood, and possibly after menopause. Performs a series of complex tasks required for the maintenance of each user, in addition to various other system requirements. Teamwork is highly valued, as is the ability to balance independent loads.

Duties and responsibilities

▫ Directs performance tuning and capacity planning activities to enhance natural assets.

▫ Oversees system architecture in order to provide redundancy in key areas and ensure overall seamlessness of experience.

◻ Performs routine back-fat checkups and assists in recovery efforts.

◻ Supervises areas of new construction and reconstruction, including but not limited to enhancement, reduction, nursing, and mastectomy.

◻ Change management skills are critical as this position experiences ups and down.

◻ Diplomatic abilities that allow for individualized treatment of each user based on her unique capabilities, changing size, and circumstance.

◻ Duties will expand at puberty to include protection services, specifically from other hormonal teenagers.

◻ Ensures ongoing programmatic excellence and rigorous support structure.

◻ Ability to retain critical focus and remain on-task for up to 12 hours per day.

◻ Serve as primary brand ambassador for comfort and support.

◻ Maintain strict adherence to brand identity in the face of trends like camisoles. Camisoles are not bras.

◻ Crisis communication skills that guarantee the user the ability to wear a white T-shirt without showing nipples. Because, God. Forbid. Nipples!

◻ Expertise in social media is critical. The Girls need to look amazing in selfies, especially when photographed from above.

◻ Ability to maintain full confidentiality is paramount.

◻ Other duties as assigned.

Qualifications

The Executive Director must be fully committed to The Girls' user experience and strategic mission. All candidates should have proven relationship management experience. Candidates should show passion, idealism, integrity, a positive attitude, and be self-directed.

Advanced degree, ideally an MBA, with at least 10 years of senior management experience; Six Sigma certification a plus; track record of effectively leading two performance-based individuals; ability to point to specific examples of having developed and operationalized strategies that have taken an organization to its next stage of growth.

Working conditions

Special working conditions include a range of circumstances such as regular evening and weekend hours, shift work, working outdoors, working with challenging clients, and so forth.

On-call responsibilities: 24/7. Travel requirement: 100%

Paid time off only at the discretion of the client, during sexy time, or on laundry day.

Physical requirements

This job is physically demanding. The incumbent will be required to continuously lift and separate a total of up to 25 lbs. each day for 12 consecutive hours or more. Requires the ability to provide ample support for standing, sitting, running, hugging, downward facing dog, and fondling, among other activities. Must be able to perform repetitive tasks with few breaks.

Apply

Please send resume and three letters of reference to hr@ ...

▫ We are an equal opportunity employer, but experience at Victoria's Secret is an immediate disqualifier

▫ Underwires need not apply

▫ Salary commensurate with experience ΔΔ

Brava!

We did not change much for 2016,
our second year.
Why would we?
The first one was perfect.

Brava!

You've all heard of John Keats and his many odes – to a Grecian Urn, a Nightingale, to Psyche. Well, were he alive today, and here tonight, no doubt he would lead us off with an ode to bras. But since he's not, we've got writer Katelynn Ulrich leading us off with An Ode to My Favorite, specifically an ode to something near and dear to the heart of all women.

AN ODE TO MY FAVORITE
by Katelynn Ulrich

You always pick me up
when I'm down
you give me a lift
when gravity conspires against me
your support is incomparable
on the days I can barely
make it to the gym,
you hold me down,
literally
I love that you understand
the beauty in simplicity
you and I don't need

to show off
but when we do
we show up
sometimes my friends tell me
I don't need you
I may not need you
but I love how perky
you make me
I love how you understand
my need for space
we spend many nights together,
but you never resent me
when I want to be alone
I adore how different you can be
sometimes you're wired,
jabbing me in all the wrong places,
but I never hold a grudge
because you were my first
rite of passage

my badge of womanhood
strapped to my chest
I wore you proudly
even if we were only training
I was on my way to woman
I walked a little taller with you
I spoke a little clearer with you
you became grounds for
bonding between sisters
you brought things together,
literally
you're with me always
in frustration, relief and pride
you're my armor and allure
my support and comfort
my first taste of power.
You are my favorite bra. ∆∆

Brava!

Every person can relate his or her life story via one object or another. Here is writer Megan Willis on her life in bras.

My Life in Bras
by Megan Willis

My life so far has been rich, full and satisfying. So have my bras. Here is our story.

Chapter 1. Breast Wishes

Before I grew a pair myself, I knew that boobs didn't just change the beholder, they changed everyone in their midst. As a young girl, I knew this was true from the reactions people had to the small bumps that suddenly protruded from my chest, and also from the way men reacted to all those super-happy girls in Playboy.

This world was going to demand that I "show it my you-know-whats," and it was during this panic-stricken revelation that I found myself at Woolworth's in the Wonderland Mall on a pre-emptive bra purchase with my mom.

I welcomed any force field, even one from a dime store, that would allow me to face the encroaching mob of adulthood and shout…

"I'll show you when I'm good and ready. Maybe never!"

The bandagey-looking bra crossed my heart, laid as flat as the heartland, and came in a cardboard box.

It was a 34 double-A with a single-hook closure and white as the virgin snow.

Chapter 2. Shock and Awe

I grew five inches and three cup sizes the year I turned 14. My "double trouble" burst onto the scene with a vengeance, launching a dressing room parade of ill-fitting contraptions that all seemed very wrong and filled me with questions with no answers. Questions like…

"Am I a hideous freak?"

"Will anyone ever like these things?"

"Am I a human being and everyone else are preprogrammed robots?"

I wondered. Ultimately, this quest for the proper cup holder revealed my perfect size: 36C, unpadded, double-hook underwire, with the straps pulled all the way up.

Support can be beautiful.

Chapter 3. Party in the Front, Table for Two

Once I learned how to dress them up and take them out, my twenties became a virtual masquerade ball of boobs; an opulent display of pomp and pageantry. Some of the brassieres I fastened upon myself were stitched-together marvels of engineering that employed pulley systems; others sheer wisps-of-things that supported many times their own weight.

There were convertibles, lacey sheers, and sporty jobs that withstood rigorous aerobic punishment. But girrrrl, it was the 80s, and as the Purple Prophet once sang, "Parties weren't meant to last." Thankfully mine did, right on through 1999.

Chapter 4. More Cow Bell

No one can prepare you for motherhood.

At 35, I gained 60 pounds while my first baby pushed my hips all akimbo and forced me to walk like T-Rex. This was just one of many wondrous and terrifying experiences to follow. Like the time I woke to the sight of my cantaloupe-sized melons spouting milk in all directions, like fountains at the Bellagio. The streams rose, and fell, in time with…

"Jane Geraldine Russell!!!" I cried out to my baby girl at 4:00a.m., "is that my pulse!!??"

I thought I might pass out, but quickly realized that I could never check out for the rest of my life. I was a mom, and I was what was for breakfast, lunch and dinner. At which point I asked myself…

"Who. The moo. Are you?"

My boobs had no answers. They were there to do a job. I had become a farm animal and I needed some heavy equipment to aid production. Something I could drop the hatch on with one hand while conducting a conference call, and still kick the dryer door closed.

Enter the industrial strength nursing bra.

If the party wasn't over before it definitely was now so I asked the late guests to kindly,

"Get the hell out!"

Size of this bra? Largest mammal on earth.

Chapter 5. You're Gonna Make it After All

At fifty-plus years of age, I'm bewildered by the sight of my own boobs but I'm just happy to still see them at all. I have two teenage daughters now, and I'm barely keeping it together in a 38 double-D, triple-hook minimizer (we're looking to downsize).

It was no one's sure bet that I'd survive this long, least of all mine, and I've always been grateful for any help I could get along the way.

Therefore, I'd like to take this opportunity to honor all my bras throughout the years, for Best Supporting Role in a Dramatic Comedy. These aerodynamically engineered fronts-pieces have given me more backbone. They've lifted me up and made it possible to be heard over the sound of my nipples, who threaten to dominate every conversation they enter into.

Thanks, Bras.

We may be riding a little lower in the saddle these days, but it's been a great rodeo. ∆∆

Braval

Some of us bloom early, some later, some never, perhaps,
but bloom is the word that gets used a lot when referring
to when women get to strap themselves into their bras.
Here is Sarah Marquise on when she bloomed.

LATE BLOOMER
by Sarah Marquise

"I think my boobs are coming," she said, and I quickly glanced down, somewhat confused.

"I figured I could trust you," she continued, "because we're both late bloomers."

I smiled, relieved. A late bloomer. I could deal with that.

In fact, my fingers were still crossed that I would remain unbloomed, forever a girl, forever only on the cusp.

I'd been hiding my own emerging breasts with a sports bra that was far too small for me.

I had faith enough to believe that if I spoke to these mountains, they'd certainly move.

Any outward womanly progress was swiftly rejected by my 11-year-old self.

"You're becoming a woman," my mother would say, and I'd cringe in humiliation, crossing my arms, frustrated that my development was unavoidable, and on display.

Some part of me, even then, understood the weight that was growing — inside my chest but outside too.

I was joining the throngs of others like me, once flat chested and free, now forever trapped behind ta-tas and titties.

But gradually, alongside the growth of my breasts came the growth of my mind.

And I grew into it all.

A form so fitted it had to be mine.

I'm a woman now, and I think my boobs are coming. ∆∆

Ah, the joys of motherhood. Kind of. Sort of. Not always, at least when it comes to what happens inside, around and about our bras. Here is writer Sandra DiNoto on that.

PROTECTING THE MILKING MACHINE
by Sandra DiNoto

After 36 hours of difficult labor with a wheezing cough (probably bronchitis) getting worse, my doctor took the nearly nine-and-a-half pound creature from me via C-section, a procedure that delays the production of breast milk.

But I was ready. I was a first-time mom committed to nursing my newborn. I had read the books, watched videos and even dragged my poor husband to breastfeeding class at the hospital.

"Breast is best" and I had invested in nursing bras.

For those of you have never seen one, a nursing bra has a pull down flap that can be unhooked, unzipped or unsnapped to expose the breast for its most amazing maternal role — to produce milk perfectly heated and nutritionally balanced for feeding and nurturing babies.

Until you experience the hunger cries of a newborn, you can't truly appreciate the value of a nursing bra, especially a model that can be maneuvered with one hand because your other arm is occupied with an agitated, hungry baby. In a matter of seconds, you have dropped the flap and your baby has latched on for feeding. The flaps can get in the way of the poor baby's suckling stance, but after a while, you both get into a pattern and figure out what works best.

But it is not all bliss.

Breasts get sore and engorged. Nursing bras should be made of a fabric that breathes and allows for fluctuations in breast size and improves breast health. A too-tight or restrictive bra can interfere with milk flow. Sometimes nipples crack, which is very painful, and bacteria from the baby's mouth enters the breast, causing mastitis, an infection of the breast tissue.

Then there are the nursing bra "accessories." No one really prepared me for the challenges of milk seepage. Yes, nursing breasts full of milk will leak, even spray milk uncontrollably. Breast milk can stain so you need disposable or washable cotton pads that can be tucked inside your nursing bra to absorb any leakage. The last thing you want to experience is being out in public and having wet spots seeping through your shirt around your nipple area.

When did it all start? According to Wikipedia, the first patent for the "nursing brassiere" was obtained in 1943 by Albert A. Glasser, and how they have evolved. Nursing bras now come with brand names. A few of my favorites are Hotmilk, Leading Lady, Decent Exposure and, get this, Bravado!

There are seamless nursing cami's and tank tops which were not around when I was nursing. I was shocked to discover that one nursing bra on the market today, Baby Sees It, has a pull down panel that reveals black and red printed images to "visually stimulate your baby while nursing." As if the breasts were not enough stimulation!

One of the most fascinating nursing bras I have ever seen but not used is the "Simple Wishes" pumping bustier which allows mom to pump "hands free" with almost any brand of electric breast pump, either double or single.

Hanging off the front of this contraption built for multitasking moms are two small bottles allowing milk to be pumped at the same time. You can get it in Amazon in pink for $27.99, a real deal marked down from $45.

According to the literature, "Enjoy no fuss and no mess with a reliable, tight seal of breast shields and flanges from our four-way layering support system. It's versatile and allows you to pump in more situations, including work, paying bills, during breakfast or lunch."

I don't know about you but who enjoys lunch while this is going on?

It's the closest I've come to finding a human milking machine, a pet name given to me by my husband when I nursed my boys. Is it any wonder why that marriage didn't last? ΔΔ

We joke about size mattering, but size does matter, particularly when we size up ourselves. Here is the writer Brenda Kilianski with a poem about size and its proportion in our lives. It is entitled Soliloquy in B-Flat.

SOLILOQUY IN B FLAT
by Brenda Kilianski

To B or not to B

That is the question my bra fitter asks me.

Why she asks I'll never know.

Isn't she supposed to be the expert?

I'm just going along for the ride.

If I go up to 34 we go down a cup size: A

It's the only time in life an A truly equals an F

But 32B?

Both letter and number seem small, insignificant

Like the bra I'm trying to buy.

I'm put off by the fact that the price of the bra

 is double my size.

But so is everything else in this department….

"There's no there there."

Said Gertrude Stein about Oakland

But she could have been talking about my chest.

Especially if she had been making this observation

Across the bay on Twin Peaks.

Mine sit like identical bottle caps.

32B.

These are my specific requirements:

No wires.

No padding.

No lace.

 "Why don't you just wear an undershirt?"

Would I get arrested for slapping my bra fitter?

Honestly, I enjoy shopping at the Macy's in Colonie Center —

I don't want to be banned for life.

So I just hit her with some snark instead:

"Clearly, what you're saying is I don't need any support?"

She smiles.

"I have seen flatter…"

She looks in another direction and I follow her glance across

the aisle to the Juniors' section.

I'm 53 and she's suggesting a training bra.

Brava!

The problem — and I grant you it is a first world problem —

Is every time I find a bra I like, one that actually fits

Be it Wacoal or Warner's or Playtex

It's immediately discontinued.

Because clearly, I'm the only woman on the planet

 who wears 32B.

I'm not a niche market

Just a nit, a bump, a cotton ball, a nub

A 32B.

To die, to sleep —

To sleep, perchance to dream: ay, there's the rub,

For in that sleep of death what dreams may come

I dream of a bra that fits.

Meanwhile, my bras, like my spirits at the moment

are old, frayed, lifeless.

I should learn to hoard them when I find one that provides

true comfort and support

Like a good friend on a bad day.

And clearly, this is one of them.

I signal the bra fitter in defeat.

"Let's try the 34A". ΔΔ

Brava!

Bras and the breasts they contain can be many things to many people, and as much as we do not want to be defined by one or the other, they can be powerful indicators of how we feel about ourselves. Here is the writer Pamela Hodges with I am Not Wearing a Bra.

I AM NOT WEARING A BRA
by Pamela Fernuik Hodges

There is only one girl in my class who wears a bra. Her name is Joanne. She has a real bra, with padded cups, thin straps and a hook in the back.

Her desk is on the far left, second from the front, by the windows that face the front of the building. Her nose is small and pointed; her hair is long, to the bottom of her bra, and parted in the center.

She is leaning over the front of her desk. I can see her run her index finger down the center of Connie's back on top of her shirt.

Her finger goes straight down; it doesn't get hooked on a strap. She is checking to see if Connie is wearing a bra. Vern and Gordon stand beside her desk. I can hear them laughing.

My nipples are flat, stuck to my chest like the pennies I put on the train tracks and made into a belt.

I sit on the far right of the room, second seat from the back, by the door. David sits behind me. He wouldn't run his finger down my back. He lends me his eraser and helps me with my math.

74

I am not wearing a bra.

I don't need a bra.

I want a bra.

Forty-six years later, I call my mom, "Mom, do you remember when I was in sixth grade? Did I ever tell you Joanne used to tease me and the other girls who didn't wear bras yet?"

"No, I don't remember."

"I must not have told you."

She didn't remember.

I did.

I avoid Joanne. At the playground I stand with my back against the brick wall and watch other children play.

When we have to line up and go back in the building after recess, I wait for everyone else to line up first. The boys line up in one line and walk in the door for the boys, and the girls line up and walk in the door for the girls. I am last in line.

My nose is round like a ball of butter. My hair is parted in the middle and comes to the middle of my back. Joanne doesn't sit close to me; maybe I can avoid her until I wear a real bra with padded cups, thin straps and a real hook in the back.

This morning, forty-six years after I sat in the same classroom as Joanne, I try to remember if Joanne ever ran her finger down my back. Did she run her finger down my back and find a strap? Did the whole class laugh at me?

And then I feel shame.

I remember.

She did.

I am not standing with my back to a brick wall. I am not last in line to walk through the girl's door after recess. My back is exposed. Vulnerable.

I can't see behind me.

I feel someone touch me.

Joanne runs her finger down the center of my back. My skin tingles where her finger touches my spine.

I am not wearing a bra.

She doesn't find a strap.

I remember because I am not wearing a bra right now. I got out of bed and came downstairs to write still wearing my pajamas. I didn't put on a bra. Sitting here in my pajama pants and sweatshirt, not wearing a bra, I am ashamed.

My back feels naked beneath my sweatshirt.

I close my eyes and I am in sixth grade again. I hear children laughing. The cars driving by the front of the school stop and the people get out of their cars and walk over to the window and look at me. Everyone in the classroom puts down their pencil and stares at me.

I am not wearing a bra. ΔΔ

Brava!

Sometimes a woman needs to rebel, and that is just what we get here from poet Shavina Richardson.

RESTRICTIONS
by Shavina Richardson

You have gone so far to restrict me that my family of origin raised me to worship you.

"Don't ever leave home without it?"

"Be sure to keep it on at night — yup, they will stay firm and won't succumb to gravity."

"They will hold your womanhood up high for the world to see."

Did it ever occur to you that your point of view was off?

Did it ever occur to you that I never wanted to be defined by YOU?

See, I've grown to discover that my strength does not belong to YOU.

I've discovered a foundation of sisters that live without restrictions.

They live their lives like butterflies with wisdom to know what direction to fly.

They live free and unapologetic — never second guessing their freedom to breast feed. Nor do they hide their bodies curves because society tells them to cover up.

They live free — just like me, and for once in my life — I'm ok with hanging-out — while hanging FREE! ∆∆

Brava!

Oh, what to tell our daughters about themselves, ourselves, as we wish for them the freedom to be themselves? One thing we do know is that some things – bras, included – are practically inevitable. Here, writer Kate Cohen muses on her daughter and the bras that await her.

A DECADE BEFORE HER FIRST BRA
by Kate Cohen

She sits in her highchair, unaware of me, transfixed beside her. She is slack-jawed with concentration; she is determined. She fails; she fails again; but she does not despair. And when my baby girl finally persuades thumb and fingers to work together in pursuit of a single, elusive Cheerio — when my baby girl triumphs — she is not triumphant. She does not pause to look at me and smile. She pushes the little round, sticky O, into her mouth and then tries again.

She does not know that this fine-motor accomplishment is the first step, the on-ramp to an increasingly difficult series of maneuvers that will one day, many endless days and a few short years from now, culminate in the ability to hook a bra behind her back. I'm guessing it will be a three-hook bra.

She'll go through a teenage period of one-hook bras and in college she'll convince herself for a while that a pretty push-up Victoria Secret thing is actually comfortable. But ultimately, when she's grown, as surely as she has my eyes and my skin, she's going to be wearing a bra that's more structural than decorative. A bra that is heaven to take off after a long day. She'll learn how to take it off without taking off her clothes. Unhook it, use one arm to pull the other arm out of its sleeve and through the bra, and then use that arm to do the same on the other side, and then pull the whole contraption through the arm hole to stuff quickly in her bag so no one sees it or her bare skin before she climbs into a sleeping bag at a slumber party.

And later, much later, she'll be able to take it off in plain view of the other women at the gym, and stretch a little, topless, because what's the big fucking deal. And then she'll wrestle some high-impact sports bra into place with a satisfying snap.

Those are gross motor skills, though. Like the ones she'll use to elbow some jerk who flicks her bra strap, or push away the boy who thinks a kiss is an invitation to explore beneath the thin fabric covering her breast. Like the ones she'll use to place someone else's hand exactly there. Like the ones she'll use to run.

But that's far in the future. For now it's fine motor she's working, her legs rigid under the table, toes flexed in whole-body focus. Her success to failure ratio is growing. The seventh Cheerio goes in. She'll be braiding her own hair with those little fingers, painting her own nails, typing a screed against makeup, applying makeup.

It will take many more Cheerios, plus page turning, crayon holding, and shoe tying, but she will one day hook that bra with ease and grace. May she do so with confidence, too, and face the mirror with acceptance and satisfaction. Or better — far better — may she not pause at a mirror even in triumph. May she simply move on, focused and determined, to the next challenge at hand. ∆∆

Brava!

Our mothers, our bras, our bras, our mothers.
Sometimes the two are inextricable in their tale of our lives,
never more so than when we age together. Here is writer
Lisa Barone with a tale of two women and some bras.

ENLISTING SUPPORT (& SOLDIERS) AT TARGET
by Lisa Barone

It's our third trip to Target for bras in as many years. Some people get support at church, others drink; we buy it in the intimate section of a chain store. Equally-new support devices line my mother's lingerie drawer at home, but we're here today, with a mission and a game plan.

"Okay, how many bras are we talking?"

"They say bras need twenty-four hours for the elastic to recover," she answers.

She's nervous so I leave the random fact untouched.

You'll be in the hospital for five days — so three? Five. We descend upon the racks; she goes left, I go right.

I resemble my mother in many ways — in coloring, in sarcasm and in stubbornness — but also as the valedictorian of over-preparing. That's why we're here. Three years ago, her undiagnosed stomach pains became diagnosed Stage 4 Colorectal Cancer.

Being here today, transports me to that day.

I remember getting the call and the vibrations in her voice. I remember her telling me I should come home; and I remember racing from Albany to Long Island to be there. I remember the hospital and I remember seeing an older woman, in a sterile bed, with tubes and machines scattered around the room.

I remember that I had never seen her that

way before. Not before cancer.

On that day, in that bed, my mother was told she would lose large sections of her colon and her liver, as well as the entirety of her spleen, her gallbladder and her appendix.

On that day, in that bed, my mother said no, not yet. She needed to go home and to prepare. She had no bras to wear to the hospital.

That's when it started. Three new bras.

"Remind me, what kind of bra do we usually get?" I asked.

The ones at home say "pantaletas."

That one I couldn't leave alone.

That's panties in Spanish, Mom.

We roam the racks, just like we've done before, reading the labels.

Women's Favorite Plunge Push-Up Bra

Lace T-Shirt Convertible Plunge Bra

Xpressions Women's Extreme Lift Bra

We acknowledge the ridiculousness of our mission, holding bras up to our matching flat chests. If Target carried something to put in the bras we'd really be onto something.

Her second surgery came almost exactly one year after the first — colon cancer in the liver. But it was good news, they said! It was old cancer, not new cancer. Old cancer signaled no additional spread — just matter they missed the first time.

Six-day hospital stay.

Four new bras.

We keep roaming. Roaming and talking. She likes my boyfriend. She wishes my brothers would move out of her house. She's sure the next-door neighbor was tickled to learn she has cancer. I tell her there's no way that's true, but it might be.

That woman next door is a bitch. I tell her about my job, my friends and my life. We talk about everything, but also nothing.

We've walked in circles for an hour.

She pauses, stops.

This sucks.

In 48 hours, she'll go back under — this time it is new cancer, and it's everywhere.

But that's then, not today. Today, in Target, we have enlisted five new soldiers — five push-ups with enough power and padding to support her through surgery, radiation and a boating accident if it comes to that. Two black, one grey, and one nude. Serious bras. We also get a black lace demi push up because, hey, she's not dead yet.

We get home and I grab her suitcase, plop it on her bed. The bras are to be packed immediately with the other items she's secured — new pajamas, new toothbrush, and yes, even new pantaletas.

Alone in her room I open her lingerie drawer to see the others. They are lined up, carefully put into place, ready for action, still there. These are the bras that have supported her before. They are firm, not having had the chance for their elastic to stretch or be pulled; reserved for a single purpose. I gently touch each one, remembering their service and the comfort they have provided.

Packing my mother's bras, in this moment, on that bed, I am happy we have so much support. Each bra in that drawer has a story and a part in helping us to prepare for what comes next. Even in these moments, when we are unsure, her bras are a tangible reminder that we walk into this battle together, ready. ΔΔ

Brava!

Can you ever achieve satisfaction with a bra? Maybe, maybe not, but chances are that a good bra fitter may be your next best friend when it comes to finding your way to a happy life in bras. Or so says Deirdre Greco.

MY TRIPLE "A" LIFE
by Deirdre Greco

Socks, no. Belts, nope. Jackets, not at all. But bras, oh my goodness, so much emotion is attached to those straps. There is a point in a young woman's life when underwear morphs into bras and panties. For some girls and young women that may be a natural and easy transition. For me it has been fraught with peril.

When I was 13 one of my problems was that I still did not really need a bra. Most of my friends needed and wore them. Jennie Clark, my deskmate, needed and wore a bra. She wore a huge bra. There were girls in my class who made fun of Jennie. I didn't. I was in awe of her.

Even the somewhat painful-looking strap marks on her shoulders seemed preferable to my complete lack of need for a bra.

My mother, who grew up in England, never understood the social and emotional toll my lack of breasts and bras was causing me. Hiding in the bathroom to change for gym, stuffing my Junior, Little Sweetheart Almost Bra with Kleenex and hoping none of the tissues fell out, was a daily trial.

Brava!

I went to Catholic school and was taught to pray for what I needed. Somehow bras and breasts did not seem to qualify for a novena. I kept hoping for help all through high school. It never came. Finally high school ended and my era began — the 60's.

The 60's ushered in bra-burning, a wonderful concept. I was able to make a political statement about freedom and feminism while triumphantly disposing of an object that had not served me well. I loved the 60's. Besides burning bras, not wearing them became a fashion statement. Suddenly I was in fashion as well as politically correct.

The 80's brought children and nursing bras. I arrived at Lady Madonna Maternity Boutique knowing that I would need some help with my selection. The salesperson called over their "nursing bra" expert.

To my horror he turned out to be Dave, the husband of one of my good friends, not someone I would ever expect to be discussing the relative merits of any sort of a bra, Dave, apparently, had no such reservations and spent at least ten minutes making sure that I knew the features that made these extremely expensive bras essential to the future health of my soon-to-be-born baby.

I was able to resist his attempts to convince me to try one of the bras on so that he could make sure the fit was correct. I bought seven nursing bras and never wore any of them as they definitely did not fit properly.

My bras faced more challenges when I had a mastectomy after being diagnosed with breast cancer at 36. Now my bra was charged with attaching a prosthesis securely to my chest. It was not always up to the challenge. On one afternoon my husband

and I were attending my daughter's gymnastic meet. We were watching from a balcony as her team warmed up on the balance beam. Suddenly my bra released my prosthesis which sailed through the air, plopping, jelly-fish like onto the gym floor.

I raced down from the balcony and managed to reach it before anyone noticed it lying there. I trusted the bra in my bathing suit to hang on and let me swim. I trusted it until the day I was swimming laps at the JCC. The woman in the lane next to me tapped me on the shoulder and asked if the breast floating in her lane was mine.

I think I have finally reached a healthy compromise with my bras and my breasts. It all still matters to me, which I sometimes wish it didn't, but I have discovered Mme. Pirie's Emporium. Mme. Pirie has an unerring eye for the correct fit of a bra.

She was horrified by what I was wearing when I came into her Emporium for a fitting. She picked my bra up with two fingers, held it at arm's length and tossed it into her trash.

She then sold me two new bras that held my prosthesis securely and fit well. Mme. Pirie and I are extremely satisfied with the two bras I purchased. ΔΔ

Oh, the feel and fit of a good bra. It's enough to inspire love, isn't it?
Opal Ingram has a little love poem about that entitled My Bra.

MY BRA
By Opal Ingram

My bra keeps me warm, I have worn so many colors
Pink Yellow Black And White Lace.
What a good fit.

A wire bra, Its loop fell out. Some new some old.
I love my nursing bra.
I had several , my bra
Held me well through
On a beach day.
Through bad days
And Good Days.
My bra held me well through my rainy days.
Through my blouse and my overcoat .
It snap In the front and some times In
The back, my favorite was one given to
Me as a gift on heart day it read my bra. ΔΔ

91

Brava!

Ah, dating. Ah, dating and our bras. Oh, the trouble we can get into with one or the other of those things, but combine them? Well? Here is what can happen with that as brought to us in a piece entitled Unruly Underwire by Denise DiNoto.

UNRULY UNDERWIRE
by Denise DiNoto

My longest romantic relationship started because I was being held hostage by a bra.

When Don first called in late September 2001 to ask me on a date, I was using a lightweight manual wheelchair. It had removable armrests, swing-away footrests and weighed less than 22 pounds. It was everything I wanted and needed from a wheelchair at the time.

The only part of the chair I didn't love was the front wheel, or caster, mount. My front casters were four inches in diameter, held in place with a fork mount allowing them to spin and rotate easily -- too easily. Things were always getting caught in them -- hair, yarn, string, even fake cobwebs at Halloween.

I don't really know how it happened. I was sitting in my bedroom, sorting laundry when the phone rang. The basket tumbled off my lap as I dashed across the floor to grab the cordless headset. Don said hello as I backed up to collect the wrinkled shirts and pants now on the floor around me.

Except, I didn't move. My front wheel was stuck, not rotating, not turning, nothing. I almost flipped backwards as I uselessly struggled to reverse my chair off the pile of clothes. Looking down I realized something was wedged into the caster fork, through the front wheel.

My pink underwire bra, a favorite because of the fit, color and comfort, had somehow become twisted up inside the wheel. The wire itself, which had been threatening to come loose from its casing for weeks, was now wedged across the wheel, effectively locking it. My attempts to move and turn had simply lodged the bra firmly in place, preventing any wheel movement whatsoever.

I sat listening to Don, wondering how to bring this up in conversation. How exactly do you tell a male stranger you are being held hostage by a bra? A bright pink bra?

"Um, excuse me Don. You don't seem like a psychopath, and I'd like to talk to you, but there is a bra stuck in my wheelchair so now's not the best time for us to have our first conversation."

Yeah — to pull that off without scaring a guy obviously flirting with me, who is interested in me, and who called me? As a rule, men didn't often pursue me, so I was not going to jeopardize a potential romantic connection just because of an unruly underwire!

I continued to talk with Don as I frantically tried to come up with a strategy to set me free. All my adult life, I have joked with friends that living with disability has made me a female MacGyver, the TV hero who could get himself out of any sticky situation. Put me in a tough spot with very few resources, and I can problem solve my way through just about anything. But try as I might, I could not release the bra from the wheel. I twisted and contorted my body, bending forward, trying to pull the strap to move the wire while still maintaining a grip on the phone.

'Yes, I love visiting bookstores."

I grabbed a pen off my dresser and attempted to push the bra out through the hole in the wheel.

"No, I haven't been to the new Barnes and Noble."

I leaned over the opposite way to take weight off the wheel praying to get it to spin freely, all the while making what I hoped were appropriate responses and encouraging remarks to Don.

"Coffee on Sunday? I think that sounds great!"

After an hour I realized the only way to liberate myself was to sacrifice the pink underwire and just cut the bra loose. I could see my scissors on the desk next to my bed, four feet away. Somehow, I had to get them.

So, I removed an armrest and used it to push the laundry basket across the floor to the desk. Turning a dirty pair of pants into a lasso, I tossed one pant leg over to the desk. The pants and the scissors slid and after four attempts, fell into the laundry basket. I dragged the basket containing the coveted scissors back to me with the chair armrest.

Snipping the offending undergarment into multiple pieces, I laughed in vindication. I wheeled backwards, taking in the tattered pink satin scraps scattered on the floor like cotton candy confetti. I wielded my shears in victory as I tossed the misshapen underwire into the trash.

MacGyver's got nothin' on me. ΔΔ

Brava!

Some bras take us to places some of us only dream of going, or such is the case with our final reader of the night, writer Sara Weeks.

THE SKIN OF MY TEETH
by Sara Weeks

Caesars Palace in Las Vegas, had for years, a luxurious showroom called Circus Maximus. Swathed in sumptuous royal purple and cream velvet, it was the site of my first audition to be a professional dancer. It was January of 1973 and on that day it was filled with 1000 women in every shape, size and ethnicity. A lavish new production spectacular called 'Hallelujah Hollywood!' was being cast for the MGM Grand Hotel being built across the street. It was to open at the end of the year.

Looking around, I saw girls garbed in flimsy bra-like tops, flesh colored fishnets and something called a g-string: a jeweled cloth triangle covering only the pubic area in front, cut high over the hip, slicing straight down their backside between both cheeks.

Their hair was pinned tightly to their heads and their makeup: pancake foundation, exaggerated eye liner over blue eye shadow topped with huge false eyelashes. Up close they looked frightening but under the stage lights, their eyes popped. Then, there was me, Nancy Nebraska, pale, plain faced, and pony-tailed, in a baggy sweater and jazz pants.

Conducting the audition was Donn Arden, the producer who'd cast the dancing Bluebells at the Lido in Paris and the Lido at the Stardust Hotel on the Vegas Strip. Now, sitting in the back of the showroom, he judged as lines of girls did the "showgirl gate" across the stage and called out to several by their first names.

"Mary Ann! Aren't you still at the Tropicana? I'm not taking anyone who's been seen before, you know that. Okay, Jeannie, you've been working the strip for years. Susan! Sorry, doll."

Also, if he pointed at you, you were out. When the herd of 500 showgirls was thinned to 100, they lined up in the wings for the pencil test. Removing their tops, a pencil was placed under each breast. If it fell to the floor, her breasts were perky, she was hired. If it didn't, her breasts were too saggy and she was dismissed.

Finally, the 75 of us auditioning for the 28 non-topless dancing jobs were called. The choreographer taught a simple routine. The music started. I'd lived for this moment, my legs flew. The first cut was made. He didn't point at me. More dancing, more cuts. Hours later, I was still in. They announced to those not in fishnets and g-strings, to get into more revealing clothing. I had no other clothes. A showgirl near me saw me panicking, handed me a two piece swimsuit and said,

"Here! They've got to see your body! Honey, in Vegas you've got to show lots of skin on stage. You can't have any scars on your face, neck, torso or legs, no weird discolorations, lop-sided boobs or stretch marks. Go change!"

I thanked her and rushed out. Snickers followed me as I got in the lineup, a vision in tangerine orange with bows. Mr. Arden, who'd come on stage, told each girl to turn around slowly as he asked her name and age. If he saw no flaws you were hired. He dismissed three in a row. Approaching me, he eyed the suit and burst out laughing.

"And what do we have here?"

I flushed hot.

"What is your name, my angel?"

"Sara."

"Turn for me, please. How old are you?"

"Seventeen."

He gasped.

"Seventeen! When will you be eighteen?"

"August", I said.

"So you're not even out of high school!"

I shook my head no and smiled.

"Wait! He said. "Are those what I think they are?"

I froze. In all the years leading up to this moment, thousands of dance lessons, classes six days a week, competing my whole life against uptight, anal-retentive ballerina pinheads, it had come to this. I'd forgotten all about them. I could only muster a sad, tight Mona Lisa grin.

"Come on, Sara. Let me see." he said.

I looked down. I was finished. Then, he took both of my hands.

"I love you already, dear heart. You have the job. But I just have to see them for myself to believe it."

I had the job! I looked up smiling from ear to ear exposing a mouthful of braces.

"So you do have them! This is a first everyone!" he said, clapping his hands. "Do you think you can get those off before the show opens?"

I beamed. "Yes Sir. I can." ΔΔ

2017

Brava!

By 2017, we knew what we had:
Pure joy. And so, we persisted.

It only seems right to start off with an overview of the bra,
a sort of personal history that makes stops along the way
at the high – and low – water marks of the personal history
we have with our bras. And for that, we've got Susan Megna,
reading Memoirs of Bras Past (By a Flat-Chested Woman).

MEMOIRS OF BRAS PAST
(BY A FLAT-CHESTED WOMAN)
By Susan Megna

Training Bra

The training bra was the start of it all

A late developer, I answered that call.

I learned from magazines and neighbor boy's jests

That I should train my body to grow large perfect breasts.

I got mom to buy me my first little brassiere.

A bandeau of cotton, with a clasp in the rear.

And though my new boobies were the size of a pea

Some discreet stuffing helped me to get to a B.

No Bra

Then came the sixties, upheaval and protest,

Women's lib seemed to circle right back to my chest.

Old ways were now quite the albatross:

"We are more than sex objects!" "Our bras will be tossed!"

My slender small stature did serve me quite well

When as bra-free rebels, we began raising hell.

Yet the worth attached to the shape of our breasts

Proved deeply enduring, lush boobs still impressed.

Nursing Bra

I moved on and started a new phase in life,

In my minimalist bra, I became a wife.

Though my love for my shape was clandestinely deficient,

To the family, my figure seemed completely sufficient.

I was pregnant or nursing for what felt like forever,

And my bra remembrance from that maternal era

Was how my plain nursing bras won my heart instantly.

They were comfortable, convenient — and I wore a cup C.

Padded Bra

Kids grew up, things changed, as did my bra desires

Being single drew me to look at padding and underwire.

Alluring promises by Playtex and Maidenform

Offered 'wonder' and 'miracles' - I felt reborn!

Although cleavage for me would still be a stretch,

I thought my Wonderbra made me quite a good catch.

Brava!

I looked in the mirror and felt amplified,

Although those bras always did take a long time to dry.

Sports Bra

My problem when exercising was never the bounce;

Chafing was the issue to be renounced.

My sports bra effectively changed that landscape.

It eliminates chafe but does nothing to shape.

Well, function over form is my newest motto,

And for sporty endeavors, you can't beat the bandeau.

A good sports bra doesn't squeeze, itch or scratch;

Basic black makes it so my workout clothes all match.

Lessons Learned Over Six Decades

Bras are a dichotomy based on how we feel

We love them or hate them — these feelings are real.

Our bodies, the styles, and personal needs,

Get mixed in with values and societal creeds.

Pricey and mostly out of view from outside,

In ugly frayed bras, we too often hide.

Yet a good one can be as good as gold

The right one can make us feel confident and bold. ΔΔ

As Susan wrote, the training bra come along early in our lives, so let's follow that up with a piece by that title by Alyssa Talanker.

THE TRAINING BRA
by Alyssa Talanker

It hung on the rack next to the real ones. Two oblong pieces of white polyester stretched between wires that hooked in the back. The lack of lace and color said it all. Ladies and gentlemen, allow me to present the unmistakable non-functional training bra.

The training bra was for all pre-adolescent girls who had no need for a bra yet. Nowhere in my 1960's teenage fashion magazine do I remember an ad for training bras. Nor do I recall seeing any pre-pubescent nymphets admiring the bosomy woman in the TV commercial for Playtex Living Bras.

One day, the training bra mysteriously appeared in my underwear drawer. I tried it on. Like the pantyhose girdle my friends and I wore which left lines on your stomach at the end of the day, the training bra was a snug fit. Who came up with this idea? Some lingerie mogul in New York City? Did his modern day grandson then inherit the business? If Wikipedia is to be believed, about 10 years ago a well-known chain department store began stocking bras for 3 to 4 year olds. Get out the baby cream.

Certainly, this invention was not the brainchild of Mary Phelps Jacobs, who received a patent for the brassiere in 1914. Before the bra, women were wearing corsets. As Mary explained to the men of the U.S. Patent Office, the brassiere gives women freedom from bones and only confines where needed. You men might especially enjoy seeing lace on a woman's bra under her sheer gown. Well, there was no lace on my training bra. I was a tomboy and dungarees were fine as evening wear.

One thing is for sure. Whoever invented the training bra was a marketing genius. Once a young girl starts wearing a training bra, there is no turning back. As she continues flipping through her latest fashion magazine, thoughts of new tops to go with the training bra suddenly enter her head. They are naturally followed by a need for new skirts to complete the outfit.

Looking back, I acknowledge some girls with maturer chests than mine at age 11 had something to put in those polyester patches. For them though, there was an AA size regular bra if they were the slightest bit wobbly. As for the rest of us tomboys, the training bra signaled the end of the hopscotch life. Our age of innocence ended much too early. ΔΔ

Another not-strictly love story about the bra come to us from the writer Denise DiNoto in her piece entitled What is Pretty?

WHAT IS PRETTY?
by Denise DiNoto

I was two hours late for work on my first day back after an unexpected five day absence due to an intense sinus infection. An emergency wheelchair repair delayed my arrival, but I was determined to make it through the day now that I was finally at the office.

So, when I began to get a strange sensation "down there" around noon I ignored it. I had been wiped out by the sinus infection and I forgot my period was due.

I had to go home to change before the situation became ugly. I called one of my Personal Assistants for help. We arrived at my home together, and I urgently threw my cape aside as I rushed to the commode.

But even when the need is great, one should not rush a transfer from wheelchair to commode. Particularly when the Personal Assistant who is working is incapable of following verbal directions. She didn't listen to my commands. She dropped me.

SNAP! I heard the crack of the splintering bone as my butt crashed down on my ankle.

Imagine the scene — me, half naked on the floor by the commode, bleeding and still needing to pee, knee blown up the size of a basketball, a whimpering Personal Assistant trying too late to make things better. And now in walks the police officer, the first to respond to the 9-1-1 call.

It wasn't pretty.

It definitely wasn't pretty as the paramedics moved me to a backboard then lifted me to a stretcher. It turned downright ugly as I swore nonstop in agony while they secured me in the rig. We don't need to talk about the ambulance ride to the hospital.

Two days later, the surgeon reassembled my fractured femur with, in his words, "a plate, screws, chicken wire and bubble gum." I asked him to point out the bubble gum on the x-ray, and was told sometimes that dissolves before imaging. The thirteen screws and eight-inch plate I will carry for the rest of my life are clearly visible.

After two weeks in a hospital bed, it was time for me to get dressed and head to Sunnyview Rehabilitation Hospital for intensive physical and occupational therapy. I was the least pretty I had ever felt in my life. I needed a shower, a razor, a manicure, and a good pair of tweezers.

My friend Sally brought some clothes, honoring my request for loose tops and comfortable pants. As she removed the items from a bag, I saw a flash of red.

"I know you aren't feeling like yourself, but I figured you'd want a pretty bra."

Brava!

Sally, bless her heart, knows I don't wear boring white bras even on the worst of days. She understands my need for color, the satisfaction I gain from knowing underneath my sensible, sexless fleece turtleneck is a scrap of satin that gives support to so much more than my breasts. Sally packed six colorful bras for me — and a tan one because she is practical, after all.

I worked harder than I ever had at any physical task for those two weeks at Sunnyview. Three hours of exercise every day, enduring the most intense orthopedic pain I've ever experienced. It was not an attractive time for me. I was angry, bitter, and resentful. I have never been an exercise person, and now I was breaking a sweat — in the morning AND afternoon! Thank goodness I had all of those bras because there was no way I was wearing any of them for more than one day at a time.

I continued therapy for months at home and as an outpatient, learning new ways to perform all of my activities of daily living. I will never recover some of the function I had before the femur fracture. I now need more assistance to complete tasks I used to do independently. So much in life has changed because of that fall in early 2016.

One thing has not changed. I still like, and wear, pretty bras. I don't wear them for a man or a woman. I'm not trying to impress or attract anyone with my colorful lingerie.

I wear them to remind myself that even when life hands me the most repulsive challenges, causing me to grimace daily and feel unlovable and homely, I am beautiful on the inside, through it all. And I deserve every color of the rainbow. ΔΔ

Here is a rare, genuine-article love story, this time from poet Opal Ingram, with her piece My Bra Blue.

MY BRA BLUE
By Opal Ingram

My bra Blue
I felt free
It held me in the stream
of my heart.

I felt tighter
When I wore it.

It cushion me well
My bra blue

It wrap around my skin
Like a good friend.
It held me tight
And I felt free. ΔΔ

Brava!

*Most women will report a love-hate relationship with
their bras, as beautifully reported here by writer
Carol Tyman in her piece entitled Underworld.*

UNDERWORLD
by Carol Tyman

Now it seems strange
I was eager to exchange
My favorite Barbie underwear
For a teeny, tiny training brassiere

And, I'd like it explained
Why my girls needed to be trained!
Would they have veered off in opposite directions
Without a Playtex intervention?

Did my burning desire to conform
Make me easy prey to Maidenform?
Or was I seeking to cover up
In hopes teasing boys would just shut up?

When I began donning shapewear
Why didn't anyone care
Enough to advise
Of all the problems that would arise?

Brava!

I would have loved to know
The list of common woes
Such as: even beautiful bras squash and pinch
With the dubious bonus of just an added inch!

It would have been grand
To learn to unhook with just one hand
While driving home from dinner or movies
Trying in vain to free my poor, trapped boobies.

And why no heads-up on challenging clothes
That standard bras never work with those?
There's a dizzying list of alternates
Backless, strapless, plunging and bralettes

Although it gave such liberation
To forego garments of foundation,
I dearly wish Physics tests
Had mentioned gravity's effects on breasts!

In my early days of mothering,
Nursing bras were quite smothering
And inept at hiding leakage
Seeping from the vicinity of my cleavage

Although they're not my favorite things,
Whether they have snaps, plaid straps, or wings
Victoria's Secret is here to stay
Because bras refuse to go away!! ΔΔ

But wait. There's more not-love-letters to the bra, specifically this one, from writer Shavina Richardson, in her piece No Longer Friends.

NO LONGER FRIENDS
by Shavina Richardson

Where Shakespeare left off...

As the late William Shakespeare noted -- "To Thine Own Self Be True"

Well how true do you wish me to be?

This form of restriction is at times too much to bare -- literally!

Sometimes digging so deep into me that I wish to depart from its very being

But so many go and have surgery to increase their cup...size—No! No, say I

For thine spine will no longer be defined. Instead you will be subjected to straps with a width that can part the red sea, and then at night when it's time to sleep without that bra...you succumb to gravity.

That extra weight is not one that you can write-off nor itemize for that credit. The only one benefiting from that daily responsibility of carrying those extra pounds is "BraVa!"

Yes, she continues to uphold her end of the bargain and supports where needed, but will never be your best friend. She is sometimes so beautiful and laced with grace, but when you consistently use her she might showcase her wire that is far from an "outliner."

I know, it appear that I'm a little bitter and don't wish to give BraVa! some love—but No! No, say I—

It has just come to a point where I no longer benefit from her support—36B to a 44DD we are no longer friends! ΔΔ

So, maybe we cannot have love for all our bras all the time, or even some of our bras all the time. But according to Jennifer Hixon, we can develop a fierce devotion to something else she wears on her chest, as told here in her piece entitled My Plastron.

MY PLASTRON
by Jennifer Hixon

A plastron is the pad a fencer wears to protect the chest, or a metal breastplate worn beneath a coat of mail, or the ventral plate of a tortoise. Mine is my post-surgical mammary compression dressing, a kind of super sports bra made of strong elastic, with a zippered front and wide Velcroed straps. Even though the plastic surgeon told me six months ago that I could wear any bra I wanted, I continue to wear my compression bra much of the time.

Part of the explanation is practical. The elastic counteracts the tendency of my breast implants to migrate toward the sides of my chest. The compression bra is comfortable because it doesn't use a band for support, and doesn't furrow my chest the way a regular bra does. But I think the real reason I continue to wear this strange garment is as a souvenir.

My mentor told me, "It's hard to find your cancer voice." If I have a cancer voice, it is the bravado I share with other people who have had breast cancer. I'm sure there are some of you in the audience. We have a wisecracking attitude toward the illness that threatens our life. We assert the "I" in the face of annihilation. I needed only surgery and Tamoxifen, but I have heard you, Sisters, shrug off your radiation, your chemo, your hair loss. Like the Amazons who legend says would cut off one breast so they could draw back their bowstrings better, we have the courage of battle.

The compression dressing is my private footnote to this public bravado. Its elastic embrace reminds me of the sweet care and attention I got when I was sick. It reminds me of the surgeons' skill. It reminds me of the soft blanket my BFF sent. It reminds me of my co-workers' gifts and well wishes. It reminds me of my brother's flowers. It reminds me of my high school friend's visits. It reminds me of the calm competence with which my husband changed my dressings and handled every other chore. It reminds me how lucky I am to be here.

And if the wide straps of my plastron should peek around the neckline of my chainmail and remind everyone of my adventure, so be it. ΔΔ

Brava!

*Amid the gamut of emotions they provoke, bras can produce fear,
especially in men, though what kind of fear and when it happens
is specific to each individual. Here is writer Dan New
with his piece Tagging Along.*

TAGGING ALONG
by Dan New

Early that morning, I waited outside the closed door of my parent's bedroom as my sister and mother conferred on a topic not meant for my ears.

Then they dragged me along on a shopping trip to Hearn's on 149th Street and Third Avenue in the Bronx. I was eight or nine. It was mid 50's. I had no idea of the secret purpose of their journey. For me, it meant the toy soldiers and trains in the store's basement, a chance to indulge my fascination with them.

We took the subway there. We walked passed Sak's and Woolworth's to Hearn's. It was getting close to Christmas. There was a dusting of snow on the sidewalks. The music of Christmas played in the streets. Lots of hustle and bustle. We revolved through the spinning doors into the lobby of the store. I looked for the down escalator.

"Not yet Danny," My mother said. She held my sister's hand as they headed toward the dreaded ladies' department, a collection of colors and fabrics that were a puzzle to me. It was going to be a long day, I thought. They continued deeper into the foreign land of blouses, sweaters and slacks then to the prom dress section and more formal evening gowns. I sighed, and slowed and dragged until my mother said, "Wait here, we'll only be a few minutes." Her voice was firm and meant not only to stay put but do not enter. It seemed as if an electrified fence had been raised. My entering would result in a stunning shock. The sign hung from the ceiling read "Lingerie". I thought, what the heck.

They were back after 45 long minutes with a small brown bag and no explanation.

"Whad'ja get?" I asked my sister. She looked away and to her mother.

"Today's a special day for your sister. It's private."

"Yeah, but whad'ya get?" I asked again. They walked silently. Until then, we had always shared our presents by a peek in the bag and a sigh that said, "I wonder what I'll get." Not today. There was a bond and I was not in it. We took the escalator to the toy department for a quick look and then the ride back home. I would glance at the paper bag on my sister's lap and try to guess, only to be rebuffed with a "NERVERMIND".

My brother was home when we arrived. We shared a bedroom.

"They took me to Hearn's shopping. I didn't get anything but Joanne got something and it's a secret. She wouldn't even let me see it."

"She got her first bra," My 13-year-old brother said.

"What's that?" I asked.

"The guys on the block call it an over the shoulder boulder holder." He smirked. I returned his smirk from my innocence like I knew. I didn't.

At dinner, we sat in our tiny kitchen. My parents, two sisters and my brother. My father bowed his head and said grace as fast as he could. Then, as was his habit, he asked, "How was everyone's day?" Then looked to Joanne. She blushed and then glanced down to her blouse where a couple of new protrusions had appeared. My mother said, "Oh Charlie!" to her husband. Her usual way of reining my father in. I looked at my mother and for the first time became aware of her breasts and her bra. I averted my glance. Silence followed. The scrapes of knives and folks on our dinner plates filled the quiet.

My Father asked my brother how his day was. "I delivered the papers, got a few new customers. I went to Barry's house to lift weights. I'm gonna save up to buy a set." Then he flexed his biceps for all to see.

"Kathy?" My younger sister faded into the wallpaper, wilting away from the attention. Two years my junior and painfully shy. "I practiced my cursive. I like the wavy lines. I'm getting better."

"Danny?"

"We went shopping at Hearn's. I didn't get anything. Joann got an over the shoulder boulder holder though." Joanne broke out in tears, my mother and younger sister gasped. I knew something was wrong but wasn't sure what. "That's what he told me." Pointing to my brother.

My brother said quickly, "I didn't say that."

"We bought her a bra, her first one. It is women's underwear. It will support your sister's breasts as she matures," my mother said. My father now gaped.

Then I asked. "Am I gonna need one?" More silence from the knives and forks erupted.

"We'll talk later," were my father's last words on the subject. ∆∆

Ultimately, our bras represent emotional and physical milestones, whether those be our acceptance or rejection of bras, the jobs they perform, their sizes or what we intend them to represent about us. Some women have one bra, some have none, while others possess dozens of them, all depending on characteristics as vastly different as sexuality to economics. But what we seem to have in common are moments in time in which we decide how we feel about the bra. Here to cover that is Sara Weeks, with her essay b..b..bra.

B...B..BRA
by Sara Weeks

Sandra Dee, Sally Field, Julie Andrews, Hayley Mills, I adored them all. Then, the summer I turned 12, I saw a movie called "Countess from Hong Kong" with Marlon Brando and Sophia Loren. Holy smoke! Sophia Loren! I didn't know they made "them" like that! Later, I sat all day peeking down the front of my shirt, pleading with my chest.

"Come on out….pulleeeeeeze…..don't be afraid…"

Nothing like hers was going on down there.

A few weeks later, on the first day of school, I was walking with Charlotte, when some boys began to act like chimpanzees, tumbling around, offering to carry Charlotte's books, asking Charlotte how her summer was. I was invisible. Once I got to the locker room, I heard whispering.

"Charlotte has boobs! She got a bra!"

She did? She does? No wonder no one was paying attention

to the knock-kneed, gangly giraffe ambling along beside her. All day long I heard a variation of the same sentence.

"Do you know who else is wearing a bra? Kathy Thorndike!"

Kathy Thorndike! The class brainiac? Oh, the humiliation…

After school, I stood in the doorway watching my mom fold clothes. Sitting down beside her I gently tugged on her bra strap through her shirt. For the life of me, I could not say the word "bra" out loud.

"Um…Mom…. when do I get one of these?"

She burst out laughing and says,

 "When you get a bust, sweetie."

Devastated, I trudged slowly to my room, cheeks flaming, thinking: "why can't I say the word 'bra'?" Is it because it's the one thing I want more than anything on earth?

That evening in ballet class, I looked around at all the girls my age. Nope, nothing going on in their higher elevations either. When I got home, there on my bed was a small rectangle box with a bra inside, size 30A, a vision of loveliness. A band-aid of loveliness, but I had my first bra. I put it in on, then gave my chest a pep talk.

 "Let's get going! You can do it!"

The next morning, I strutted up the street. I felt like a movie star. But no one asked to carry my books.

Joey, the cute, new boy in our neighborhood, breezed past me on the street. At school, I heard no whispers.

Two years went by. Still no activity in the north country. Washed so many times, my Band-aid of loveliness looked like a rubber band. In ballet class one evening, I noticed Mrs. Krasnoff, who owned the studio, standing in the doorway watching me. When she wasn't the instructor she sat and observed.

Just before summer break, I was told to come to her office. She asked in her thick Russian accent,

"Sara, you're 14 now?"

I nodded.

"Good. How would you like to go to New York next year?"

New York! She told me I was to begin training with her in the fall in the solo parts in "Gisele" then the following spring, audition for George Balanchine of the NYC Ballet.

I squealed, "Yes, I would love to!"

My parents were summoned and thrilled with the news. But now it was summer. Aretha Franklin, The Young Rascals and Paul Revere and the Raiders, blasted from my AM radio as I baked every day out in the glorious warmth. But as fast as it arrived, summer ended, I turned 15 and it was September. At my first regular ballet class of the season, the dance studio was overflowing with ballerina penguins walking around with perfect turnout greeting one another. I said "hello" to Mrs. Krasnoff and walked over to the barre. Suddenly she shouted,

"Sara! Come here this instant!"

Hesitant at her sudden anger, I took a few steps toward her.

Brava!

Her face contorted, eyes bulged out,

She was visibly unglued.

"What did you do? You've ruined everything!"

Confused, I couldn't speak. Then…I quietly asked,

"Am I too tan?"

She gestured wildly. "Look at you!"

I looked down at my arms, legs, clueless. She then spoke in a low, growling snarl.

"You weren't that size in June. What size is your bosom now?"

"Oh! A 36C."

"Good God!" she rasped.

My trip to New York -- over. I hadn't known this about ballerinas, but companies prefer them flat-chested.

However, to me it didn't matter because Sophia Loren and I now had a sacred bond, because now I had upper peninsulas, too. And……

The next morning, on the first day of school:

"Why yes, Joey, you may carry my books." ΔΔ

Brava!

Who are we in our bras? Are we all the women we've ever been there in our cups, or when we wear a sports bra, are we our athlete selves, shedding our corporate or writer or doctor selves for a while? How does each bra define us, if it does? Here is Diane Cameron with an essay entitled That Essential Girl, to shed some light on those ideas.

THAT ESSENTIAL GIRL
By Diane Cameron

A little booklet called "You Are a Young Lady Now" got me into trouble when I was 11 years old. My mother had given it to me, and she told me that I wasn't to share it with other girls—that this was something for their mothers to deal with.

It was the most vague and euphemistic booklet with pictures of happy, pony-tailed teenaged girls doing fun and active things, and it had drawings of pretty Fallopian Tubes flowing gracefully somewhere in the human body. In the drawings, the lovely tubes didn't connect with any body parts that might have led to "What goes where?" and "How does that get in there?" questions. Kimberly-Clark was leaving that up to the mothers.

But knowing that this info was somehow related to sex, and noting that my mother said I could not share it with girls, I took the booklet to school and I rented it for 5 cents a read to the boys.

I had plenty of customers. The boys in my class were as naïve as the girls about sex and bodies. My best buddy, Ervin Bauman, and I walked to school together every day and we spent hours speculating on how kissing after you got married could make you pregnant but kissing before marriage did not. We obviously had not learned to count backwards from nine like my mother and the other neighbor ladies did when someone had a baby in the first year of marriage.

So, this booklet had clues. It was hot property.

What I remember most fondly about that time was how it felt to be that girl. I was a girl who took information about her changing body and found opportunity. I assumed that menstruation meant not more restriction, as my mother probably had in mind, but I envisioned the sailing, swimming, and horseback riding that the Kimberly Clark pamphlet seemed to promise.

But what I most wanted that year was a bra. The 6th grade girls were getting them. I'd seen my sister's bras, and I saw ads for bras in the ladies' magazines that my mother read.

There was a special charge to bras — kind of like that Kimberly Clark booklet. Bras too had something to do with sex, and something to do with power. I leaned in.

I think of that 11-year-old when I hear the outcry about referring to women as girls. It belies what we know about girls, and what they are really like. At 11 I was brave, outspoken, active and bossy, and yes, entrepreneurial. The girls who were my friends were honest and bold with each other. We said, "I won't play with you if you are mean." And "I don't like you when you do that." Yes, then like most girls we hit our teens and became self-conscious, body conscious, and kind of emotionally unconscious.

I wanted a bra just so the straps would show. I didn't actually want breasts — I was a gymnast and a dancer — a slim physique was deregiur. But I wanted a bra.

I had to wheel and deal to get my 27, double-A ivory satin brassiere. There was nothing to go in it. The AA the cups were empty and wrinkly. But I wanted straps, not understanding that bras also suppress, depress and cover over girlish fierceness.

Over the years I've bought lots of bras: stretchy bras, sports bras, underwires and padded bras to look good in my clothes; I also bought bras to be worn with no clothes —Yep, those are the real power bras.

Now older, my body changes again. I fight the tendency to think that my bras don't have to be nice any more. But I remind myself to stay close to that subtle power. I want to reclaim that girl. The best way that a grown woman can come into her own is by circling back to who she was at 11 or 12. To that essential girl.

So as a feminist in my 60's I'm OK with being a girl. It's the best model I can think of for a woman who embodies fun and fierceness, courage and kindness, curiosity and daring. I'm still all about pretty bras, and I'm still going for the girl. ΔΔ

Brava!

*Our adult selves relate to our bras both directly and indirectly,
of course. In Susan Comninos's poem, Childlessness, the reference
to a bra is almost tangential – fleeting, but present.
See if you catch it as it ghosts by.*

CHILDLESSNESS
by Susan Comninos

Per il mio ex amore

I guess it's an affectation:

The boat you slip into

When you flee the night. The sea's

Awake with insulin. What does it mean

That I dream of you, still

Crossing palms, lawns, the laws

Of language suspended? Drop your accent

On a female line of wash.

Pin me in place. Your

Wine from old grapes

And men in shirtsleeves

Keeps me sick on morsels

From another life: parchment; wafers

Like paper; loss. How

I loved you in your derelict

Boots; your sweat

-Stained limbs; your

Rancid misuse of a

Horse. As my time

For a child fled, you

—*il mio dolce codardo*—

Thought bride and bridle

Fit the same. ΔΔ

And so, we've run the gamut of the bras in our lives and the times and phases they represent. Let's wrap up this year's contributions with a series of what writer Tina Lincer calls Braku – haiku rounding up the bras in her life. Here is a collection entitled Down to the Wire: 18 Braku.

DOWN TO THE WIRE
by Tina Lincer

Pointless

These small gals weren't

born to shimmy; my trainer

bras walked off the job

Rite of passage

Boys will be boys, twang

and snap! Another bra strap.

7 th grade soundtrack

Cotton balls

"You're padded!" "I'm not!"

"Liar!" They're right. Why confess

about the stuffing?

Brava!

At 16
Nineteen seventy one
Times a changin', bra comes off
Freedom for the girls

Moody, prickly, tense,
Bralessness: perfect fit for
this teen in revolt

To every bra, burn
burn burn. This undergarment's
now politicized

Mortification
One string bikini
Little tits, big ocean wave:
One-piece, evermore

Oppression
Whose sick idea was
it to wire up our bra cups?
The Grand Torturer

Parity
Underwire jock

Brava!

straps for the boys? And why not?
That's Victor's Secret.

New bride
Lovely lace beckons
I'm leaving the no-bra zone
Farewell to my youth

The power of two
My bra has become
A cover-up, a come-on
Dual booby trap

Peak moments
Making mountains out
of molehills is a job for
fully padded bras

Love and nourishment
Anything look worse
than a nursing bra after
A feeding frenzy?

Bra shopping
Anything feel worse

Brava!

than try, try, trying on a
forest of ill-fitting bras?

Laundry day on the campground
Colorful wet bras
hang on branches near our tent
Silky ornaments

Namaste
Behold the T-strap
bra for yoga class. Call it
my halter ego

Count on it
Bras are like Swiss bank
accounts; hidden assets much
Appreciated ΔΔ

Brava!

2018

On this day,
our fourth BraVa,
there is a different tone,
a feeling in the air that
we can almost see.
All of us are more aware than ever about
the power each of us possesses
and how that power is used.
As a result,
there are far fewer love stories to the bras
than in previous years,
and more of those about that power –
the lack of it,
the relinquishing of it,
the seizing of it,
the owning of it.

So, sit back, but do not relax.
You are in for a meaningful
night of storytelling.

Wearing a bra is a commitment that begins early and lasts a lifetime.
And in that, it is a unique relationship in the life of a woman.
Here to take that on is Christine McCue reading
The Biggest Gamble a Woman Can Take.

THE BIGGEST GAMBLE A WOMAN CAN TAKE
by Christine McCue

A woman and her bras are about as close as two things can be. Not because of their physical proximity to one another. Nor because of the precious cargo which they hold. Bras are special because when a woman finds a good one[1], she holds onto it as dearly as if it were family; maybe, perhaps, more dearly than family itself. With the divorce rate at 50%, one could argue that family comes and goes, but a good bra — that's forever love.

Sadly, when you're buying a bra you don't know whether it's going to be a good bra or, instead, a demonic torture device like the 57 fiendish bras you have stuffed in the back of your underwear drawer that you only take out if you are strapping it on a voodoo doll of your boss.

They're the bras that pinch and poke and scratch and gouge. I only wear those when I donate blood. It saves the Red Cross nurses a lot of effort. They just hook the blood draw up to any one of the plethora of open wounds.

If you're like me, when you bought those satanical containment contraptions you had the highest of hopes. You thought that perhaps you would stumble upon some heavenly designed brassiere surely created by the Gods of Olympus themselves. You brought it home, tried it on[2], and quickly learned that your dreams of unmolested, full-frontal support were dashed — yet again. Why do we let ourselves engage in such a fantasy time after time, ladies?

Buying a new bra is the biggest gamble a woman can take other than saying "I do". Thus, when you finally find a bra worthy of your adoration, you worship said bra. You may even talk to your bra when you take it off at night, or possibly sing it lullabies, or perhaps name it — "Ying & Yang," "Lucy & Ethel," or simply "Congress" (your bra, after all, is bicameral). Your bra almost becomes a part of you, especially after you wear it for three days straight –- which you must, because in your entire lifetime you have only found two good bras. If you do the math, that leaves one day out of the week that you must wear a sports bra. Ah yes, the sports bra. Wrapped so tight that the Chinese foot binders of old would be envious.

I don't know if guys have such an issue with their foundation garments. Fellas, is it difficult to find good undies that keep all the furniture in the same room? ΔΔ

---

[1] Defined as: fits right, straps don't fall off the shoulder, cute, and comfortable.

[2] Who wants to try it on in the store?

Brava!

Along the road to that bra commitment is the training bra, followed by many bras along the way. Sometimes there is an interruption to the order. To cover that, here is writer Mary Scanlan with her piece, Just Like All the other Girls

JUST LIKE ALL THE OTHER GIRLS
by Mary Scanlan

"But all the other girls have one," I whined to my mother for almost a year. It was in the mid-fifties and I was a flat-chested teenager longing to look like the girls I knew.

I was taller than most of my friends and slimmer than most, with red hair. Not exactly a curvy blond like so many of my friends. Adolescent self-esteem depended on my wearing a bra, or so I thought, embarrassed that I wasn't like everyone else I knew. But, I was being guided by my old-fashioned mother, a decade older and more conservative than the hip mothers I thought all the other girls enjoyed, who didn't discuss any body part or function with me.

Finally, Mother relented and she and I went to her favorite specialty store in New York, Best and Co., where we had haircuts and bought clothes for special occasions, and where she knew the saleswomen and they her. I always believed she was embarrassed by the conversation she had with them about her daughter's desire for a bra. They, of course, were perfectly professional.

One came with me into the fitting room with a couple of samples — without Mother. We left the store with white cotton bras, one step above undershirts in their design and function. No wires, no fancy details, no lace, just plain old brassieres with simple straps and a hook in the back to keep it all together. I don't remember any flexibility to tighten or loosen either the straps or the back hook. They were, indeed, just another version of an undershirt, but ended at the base of the chest rather than at the waist.

Happily, as I matured and married and had children, my chest grew from a 32AA, after my first child. The nurses in the hospital where I first gave birth had a good laugh at my small breasts attempting to nurse our baby. The laugh was on them when I successfully nursed her for the next year, growing fuller as the year went on.

More than forty years later, my chest became an issue again. I was hit in a car accident that left me with 24 fractures on my legs and right arm, and in my chest, spending 175 days in hospital and rehab. I don't remember most of the hospital time, but do remember the last three months in rehab, spending each day learning how to walk, dress and feed myself again. I arrived there with casts on both my legs and my arm. One by one over the weeks, we took off the casts until finally, when I left rehab, I could carefully feed myself and walk with great assistance.

Feeding myself was a chore and took a long time each day. And so did dressing. Getting on socks and shoes was a gigantic effort at stretching my body into a sit up and engaging my hands to reach my toes. I learned tricks to get my feet in a certain way to put the socks on more easily and then wriggle my feet into my shoes. But nothing was as difficult in as putting on and hooking my bra. I was always uncomfortable when there was a male aide helping me, watching me jiggling the bra around my boobs. Female aides were understanding. We usually giggled as I struggled with the bra, cursing the hook in the back and often relenting to the aide's assistance.

I went home from rehab able to walk with assistance, and challenged each day to get dressed and undressed, and to eat. The physical therapy aides, who came a couple of times each week, spent many an hour on exercises and stretches for my arm and hand, focusing on by ability to feed myself, to use my computer or open jars. Only when I asked did we carefully wrench my arm behind my back to close or open my bra. I learned to secure it in the front and twist it so that the cups were covering my breasts and the hooks cheerfully clamped in the middle of my back. That was never a comfortable or welcome moment as I fumbled with humiliating lack of ability. But, suffering wants to teach you something.

There came the day, not unlike the one at when I was fitted with my first bra, that I gained control of the hook and joyfully opened and closed my bra with my right hand leading my left. Such bliss! Such a feeling of accomplishment! I wished my mother were there to embrace it with me. "See Mother," I'd say, "now I can be just like the other girls." ΔΔ

*Mothers and daughters have many links, though one of the
fundamental bonds is over, through and around our breasts and
our bras. Here is Denise DiNoto with a tale entitled Playtex 8267.*

PLAYTEX 8267
by Denise DiNoto

Whenever I am shopping in the lingerie section of a store selling Playtex bras — the ones sold in the plastic containers with
the blue or pink cardboard — I always look for model number
8267, the 18 Hour Original Comfort Strap Wirefree Bra. 34 C is
apparently a popular size because rarely do the stores have it in
stock. If I am lucky enough to stumble upon the coveted size and
model, I whip out my phone and call my mother.

"Mom — you still wearing a 34C? It's the 18 Hour one, right?
I'm in Boscov's shopping for bras and I looked at the Playtex ones
for you. They only have it in white; is that alright?"

The call is really just to let her know to expect a new bra in the
mail. Of course my mother, Caroline (or Dolly as she is known
to everyone), is still wearing the iconic Playtex 18 Hour Bra! It's
the only style of bra I have ever seen her wear in my 45 years of
life. At 91 years old, Dolly is not about to change something as
critical as her trademark bra.

Dolly's bra, like her, is no-nonsense and genuine. It is functional without needless frills. It gets the job done in a superior manner without calling attention to its work and craftsmanship. No excess lace or color is necessary for her brassieres. Although the model now comes in a variety of colors, you won't see Dolly wearing any colors other than white or natural beige.

As a child, I noticed the other neighbors only put sheets and towels on their backyard clotheslines. However, Dolly's underwear and lingerie were displayed for all to see as they dried in the breeze. Of course, so were mine when I lived at home since I was physically unable to do my own laundry. This didn't seem odd to me because Dolly never used her clothes dryer then and only rarely uses it now. Two days before I left home to be an exchange student to Australia at age 16, I posed for a photo in the backyard with my parents. Dolly sent the photo halfway around the world to me and I promptly put it on the dresser in my borrowed room, in a borrowed frame my host brother gave me. Not until he asked me why we had posed before laundry did I realize Dolly's five bras were waving in the wind behind our smiling heads. The photo spent the entire year with me, on display in each host family house — me, my parents and Dolly's bras. Today it is on the first page of my 4 photo albums from that magical year Down Under.

A few weeks ago, I told my mother I might write this essay about her and her bras. I wanted to know if she would be comfortable with me sharing what some would consider personal information with strangers.

"Well, I suppose if anyone can find a way to make my dull white bras interesting, you can. Remember, I wear the 18 Hour

— not the Cross Your Heart."

Was she telling me I was shirking in my bra shopping? Had I made a mistake and accidentally purchased the wrong style? I went online to verify I had purchased the right bra and made a shocking discovery. In 2015, Playtex had a rebranding and changed the model number and name of their iconic bra. It is now model number 4693B, known as the 18 Hour Ultimate Shoulder Comfort Wirefree Bra. I called her again, wanting to make sure she had this important update and also to verify she had sufficient quantity. Apparently I had been neglectful in my duties.

"I'll still wear it! I have 4 right now so I'm good. I rotate them in my drawer after I do the laundry so I don't keep wearing the same one all the time. That way they last longer."

Even though it has been years since I've sent a new bra to my mother, she is still treasuring the past gifts I've given her; taking care to keep them in good condition for a little longer until life permits me the time and energy to resume my regular lingerie shopping. Simple life lessons from Dolly. Who knew so much could come from a bra? ΔΔ

What does our bra actually do for us? Just ask writer Opal Ingram,
and she will read her poem, The Bra.

THE BRA
By Opal Ingram

My bra was around my skin
Like a good friend it held
me tight
and free I stood brave when
I first got it

It was soft in a shade
of a bright blue.
It held my chest well
I look good with my bra

It made me feel well and blue
I Took it off and threw it in the
Air and it did not even tear.
My bra wrap around
Like a good friend It held
Me up
I walk around lifted
And free
It held me in the stream of
My heart felted so good
I wore it
It cushioned me well
my it wrapped around
My skin like a good friend
it held me tight and
I felt free. ᴧᴧ

There is a sisterhood of the bra, no doubt about it.
And to report from the front lines of that sisterhood is writer
Tina Lincer with her piece, Sis-Boom-Bra.

SIS-BOOM-BRA
by Tina Lincer

I like to give my sister things. She's frugal to a fault, an anti-consumer, an uber-minimalist, a lovable eccentric. At 67, for the first time in her life, she lives alone in our Queens childhood apartment after caring for our now deceased parents for — well, forever.

When I visit, I bring my sister shoes. Sneakers, actually. The ones she owns are 20, maybe 30 years old. Though she doesn't complain about her frayed footwear, I eagerly pass along my daughter's castoffs. Giving my sister gold lamé Polo lace-ups makes me feel I'm adding a pop of color to her otherwise pared-down life.

I bring my sister socks, lots of socks, to go with her gold sneakers.I bring tote bags. My sister loves bags. I bring hotel shampoo samples. Ditto. I bring dishtowels, bath towels, sheets and blankets. All have seen better days. My sister oohs and ahhhs over every item, greatly appreciative of these freebies. She buys nothing for herself. Ever.

One day, I bring my sister a bra. She had, in fact, asked me for this.

"Got any extra bras?" she casually said, as though I had dressers full of Maidenforms and Vanity Fairs to dispense.

I had to think — did I? Surely I had something, I reckoned, especially when I realized that the last bra my sister bought was likely during the Regan Administration.

Suddenly I was cleaning out my dresser drawers. This bra purge felt good. Who needed these old things?

My sister did. To replace her even older things.

I started with a basic item, wireless and white, gently worn. My size was her size, I guessed.

She loved it.

Before long, I was stuffing envelopes with my old bras and sending them through the mail. But then I began to wonder: Was this weird? Was it truly unmentionable?

Maybe I should have realized sooner that my sister needed bras. I remember a conversation, years earlier, during one of my visits to Queens. While walking to my car, we passed the clotheslines in a courtyard behind the apartment. In the fading autumn light, only a few socks and shirts were pinned for drying. Once, the drying lines were full with my family's and the neighbors' shirts, pants and pillowcases.

"Do you ever hang your wash anymore?" I asked my sister that afternoon.

"Never," she told me. "It's disgusting. The birds come and crap all over everything, and once they took my bra."

I kept walking. In one swoop, she'd destroyed my image of

the beautiful laundry of my youth dancing al fresco on the lines. Urban bra bandits! Who knew? Avian crooks on a low-flying mission to steal my sister's bra.

Maybe my sister's been missing that very bra for ages.

The fact is, though she and I have never been close, and we've too often been unkind to each other, what woman doesn't need a new(ish) bra — especially a woman like my sister, who never left home but fled her job; who never married or had kids but took intimate care of our dying mother; who rarely ventured more than a few blocks beyond the rooms we were raised in?

My sister has no chance of getting a new bra unless I bring her one. She doesn't drive, and the shopping avenue she walks to doesn't include clothing stores. Can you buy a bra in CVS? Even if you could, it's not happening. My sister's natural frugality rules the day. She set the trend for minimalism before the hipsters pounced on it.

But I'm not here to judge. My sister makes her way in the world in her own quirky fashion. Life's a spectrum. We all fit where we fit.

Which brings me back to this bra business. I've got an extensive designer bra collection while my older sister hasn't had a new bra in decades. And it occurs to me that since participating in this BraVa event, I've given new bras to many strangers these past few years.

So here's an uplifting thought: I could buy my sister a brand new bra and be — need I say it? — a super supportive sibling. ΔΔ

*Men and bras have a long and varied history. But here is
a take on bras you have probably never heard before. It's from writer
Dan New and it's called, Back in the Day.*

BACK IN THE DAY
by Dan New

"Danny! Get up here, right now!" My mother's voice called down from our third floor Bronx apartment. It was the close of summer, only a week before school would start again. Butch, Eugene and I had frayed the nerves of many adults on our block by then. My usually quiet mom had reached the end of her rope based on the shrill in her voice. It was the late 50's, I was 12 years old.

I climbed the stairs, slowly.

"Get in your room, stay there until your father gets home." I slithered past her in the narrow hallway and planted myself on the corner of my bed, my feet dangling just above the linoleum floor. I pondered my fate then began daydreaming before I imagined myself walking on the ceiling through our home, my way of calming the anxiety of waiting.

In an hour, my father walked through the front door. I heard his footsteps followed by a short inaudible chat with his wife. My bedroom door opened. My father, still dressed in his New York City bus driver uniform, filled the doorway.

He opened one of the drawers of my blonde veneer dresser. He reached in and pulled out a brassiere, white, elastic and stolen.

"Where did you get this? He asked.

"I never saw it before." I said.

"It's in your drawer."

"Maybe it got mixed up in the laundry."

He shifted his weight to his other leg as he lit a Pall Mall. I knew this wasn't a good sign.

"Let's try this again. Where did you get this?" He demanded.

"It's not mine." I stalled.

"It's in your drawer."

"I'm holding it for someone."

"Who?"

"I can't tell you."

"Oh, you're gonna tell me."

"It's Butch's." I lied.

"Wait right here." And he was gone. Ten minutes later, he returned with Butch and Butch's father who lived on the fifth floor of our building.

"Butch, is this yours?" My father asked. Butch looked to me.

"Don't look at him," said Butch's father.

"Out with it, you two."

"OK," Butch started. "We were up on the roof."

"You're not allowed on the roof," his father said.

"We were there. OK?" Then continued under his father's glare.

"The laundry was hanging on the lines drying. We started running through it. It was fun. One time I came out of three rows of sheets and that was hanging on my arm. Eugene said it was Mrs. Diamente's."

"Hold on, Eugene was there too?" my father asked. Butch nodded.

"Wait just a minute," my father said, and again left the room. He returned with Eugene and his mother. They lived on the fourth floor. The space grew crowded and hot. My mother now stood in the doorway, listening.

"When did this happen?" my father asked.

"A coupla weeks ago," I said.

"And you been hidin' it ever since?" Eugene's mother asked. "What for?"

"Well, it's a really good slingshot," I said. Eyes rolled. "HUH," my mother grunted. I noticed a wisp of a grin on Butch's dad's face. "Explain?" my father asked.

"Well, it's the elastic. We'd take turns. It took three of us. Two to hold the ends and the other guy to load the egg into the pocket," I said.

"It's a cup," Eugene's mother said. "A cup for christsake."

"I wondered where my eggs went," my mother said.

"So, where did you launch them?" my father asked.

"From the roof," Eugene and I said in an echo.

"Five floors up, at what?"

"We just shot them, sometimes two at a time, you know, both cups."

"Did you hit anyone?"

"Don't know, we'd just run after we shot them. I'm thinkin' maybe cars parked in the street," Butch said.

"Wait here."

150

The adults left for the living room. We sat in silence. They huddled then reentered.

"Here's the deal. The three of you are gonna wash and wax our cars. If anyone tells us they were egged then you do the same to their car. Got it?" We nodded.

"One more thing. You've got to return Mrs. Diamente's bra to her. All of you. Today."

She was my next-door neighbor. We walked the hall. I rang her bell. She opened her door.

"Mrs. Diamente, we found this on the roof, thought maybe it was yours."

Her hand reached out and retrieved it. She closed the door without a word. ΔΔ

This year we have a featured artist. Her name is D. Colin and she is a poet of real renown. Here she is with her piece, Soutien.

SOUTIEN
By D. Colin

When I was eight years old,

I played a game of house with my cousins.

All braids and bright eyed, I was the only girl in the room.

I don't remember why I had to

but I started to change my clothes

There I was bare/flat chest/shirtless

when my mom walked in the room

and before I could say sorry,

I was on my knees, shirt demanded

back on my body, snot faced and kneeling until my dad came

home. I learned my first gendered lesson that day: that boys

could bare their chests and girls could not. That I had to cover

a temptation I didn't know I possessed. That I couldn't play

a boy if I was ever playing house again.

When I was ten years old, I got my period for the

first time. My mother told me to stay away from
boys except I was already thinking the boys don't want
me pimpled/dark skin/nappy headed/ugly

When I was eleven years old, my mother took me shopping
for my first soutien. In French it literally means support.
I only ever knew it to mean bra in Kreyol
I knew a girl who already had melons.
Mine were more like grapes
Thought maybe that's why they're called training bras...
they train grapes to be melons...?

When I was sixteen, I was still waiting
for my mother's inheritance. I didn't know how many
cups larger, just knew mine were less than half full than hers
We shared food, sometimes a skirt, we could share a laugh
but we'd never share a bra
My itty bitties were still training
They had only ever learned to be peaches

and I was told to zip all the way to the top
that all the buttons on a shirt are there for a reason
so I'd hush my peaches up under loose plaid shirts
lest the loudness of their sweet attract flies
I used to think about the women in Haiti

bare breasts and bathing/shifting freely beneath a shirt
How mine weren't large enough to worry for
that I had been more Colin than Danielle
A boy protecting myself from boys
How a soutien never supported me that way
How it's only function was to cover them up twice
Soutien, D. Colin
How it only ever stopped them from dancing

Now that I'm thirty-six
I know I don't get my chest size from the
women in my family. I used to think it was a curse
and now I hold my cup all full in my hands
I've been training them all my life to restrain themselves
To talk less
To not show up or show off
When I've only ever wanted them to be free
Like that little girl
All braids and bright eyed
Being anything that she wanted even if it was a boy
Instead of protecting herself from them all ΔΔ

We all have a secret life with our bras, one we negotiate as we go through life. Here is Jill Bryce with some insight on that in her piece, Image of Support.

IMAGE OF SUPPORT
by Jill Bryce

Robin was all dressed for her part-time job and even had the cheap, rotten bra on.

"I really have to wear it, as bad as it."

The brassiere had been her sister's Jasmine's and was handed down to Robin and her 38 C breasts a couple years ago. She had to admit, the chintzy bra offered a tiny bit of support for her voluminous bosom, or as she called them Baps, among dozens of other names.

Robin was creative and also named her breasts, Julie and Suzanne. They kept her company, like old familiar roommates.

The bra was originally white, but after two half year of wear, it was dingy and spent, a shade of gray and torn in the left cup.

Robin's moods went up and down with the condition of her bra. With a supportive bra in good condition, she was optimistic. The dirty old bra drove her way down in the dumps.

"I'm saving for a new bra. But it's gonna be a while. I have to pay my heat, water and electricity, so many bills, and my with my mother's bills too, it's all too much," she said to herself.

She walked to the bus stop and sat down on the bench to wait for the bus.

Some of the people who encountered Robin often heard her talking to herself about brassieres. She jumped from topic to topic — usually about bras. Now she was telling about Mary Jacob, a New York socialite, who received patents for inventing the modern bra. Jacob used two handkerchiefs and a pink ribbon to create the first design to be widely used. Robin said Jacob eventually sold the patents to the Warner Brothers Corset Company.

She said feminists protested the 1968 Miss America pageant calling bras "instruments of female torture." The protesters couldn't burn their bras because of police. Instead they threw the bras into a garbage can, but the "bra burners" label stuck.

Robin was often talking to herself about bras

Well girls. How did you sleep?

I had a great night sleep; at night we are free of that nasty cheap bra, said Julie.

I dread getting into the ratty, old, torn bra. It does nothing for me, said Suzanne. And when I wear it, I'm sagging, like a breast twice my age.

Don't felt bad, I often dangle near Robin's belly-button, said Julie.

When the bus finally came, Robin lept onto it.

As luck would have it, the force of the move make her bra collapse.

Her old faithful, front closure bra, which can even make large boobs looks perky, was no longer supporting the Peaks.

"Now what am I going to do?"

Robin couldn't go to work looking like this.

The girls, Julie and Suzanne, were startled when the hook holding the melons broke. What a jolt, said Julie. I thought we were going down.

Robin was distressed; her boobs were hanging out like the wind. She was embarrassed and humiliated.

Suddenly she found help.

She spotted a small ad on the bus for wholesale bras down at Leonard's Discount Shop. It just a couple bus stops away. She counted her money, including her hidden stowaway cash, for an emergency like this .

"Well girls, I've got to buy a new brassiere."

The girls were giddy, or so Robin imagined.

The store owner checked on Robin as she tried on an array of bras. She noticed the old bra was falling apart. "I see you're having problems with your old bra. I'm going to give you 50 off on the new brassiere," said the store owner.

Robin was overjoyed by her good fortune. "A new bra. It's like a new beginning. A bra can have a big impact on my mood."

"Happy Days Are Here Again," popped into Robin's ear and she sang it and imagined Julie and Suzanne singing along.

Other patrons in the store were starting to sing along: "The skies above are clear again…" ΔΔ

Men intersect with bras in various ways. Here is a piece from Grace Pell entitled Confessions from Corsetry, that illustrates one of those ways.

CONFESSIONS FROM CORSETRY
By Grace Pell

I was 18 in 1966 and working part-time to put myself through college in the Women's Foundations and Corsetry Department at Sears. My badge said Miss Bone. Coming from a family of seamstresses, I comfortably sported the tape measurer around my neck and I was the consummate professional in taking careful measurements to assure a correct fit.

To calculate bra band size, measure below the breasts keeping the tape taunt and straight, then round to the next whole number. If the rounded number is even, add 4 inches; if odd, add 5.

For bra cup size, measure the fullest part of the bust keeping the tape parallel to the floor around the body, then subtract the difference between that measurement and the band measurement. If the subtraction produced a one-inch difference, the cup size was A; two inches, B, etc.

After a customer tried the size indicated by the tape measurement, we would be ready to bring alternate styles or sizes to the fitting room. As the woman who trained me said, "If their cups runneth over, get them a larger size. Don't let them leave here bulging out of their bras."

If the customer didn't want to believe they were really that big, we said, "Forget about the size, how does it feel? Is it comfortable? Some manufacturers just run smaller than others."

Unlike in the Women's Dresses Department, we were strictly forbidden from any touching to assist with zipping, hooking or adjusting undergarments.

For a pre-teen purchasing her first training bra, I was taught to demonstrate on myself like a flight attendant readying for flight, pretend-hooking the bra in the back and bending over at the waist, lifting and pulling myself fully into the cup and finally adjusting the straps to snug them, like the flight attendant pulling on a face mask.

Certain women could wear more bra styles than others. Like belly buttons with innies and outies, nipples could be inverted or everted. Inverts could wear any bra style comfortably. But Everts needed some padding to assure they wouldn't spike out distractedly in a cold breeze. For Everts who wanted to wear a thin comfortable bra, Sears sold flesh-toned adhesive "privacy petals." Customers complained when they depended on these pasties, but then perspired, causing their petals to wilt.

Some customers wanted to bulge out of their bras. That was their definition of a perfect fit. They wanted push-up bras, which we sold with every other type of bra imaginable: sleeping bras, nursing, minimizer, training, some fitted with folds to secure a prosthesis. One day, I heard a woman swearing trying to fit herself into an "all-in-one" girdle and corset.

"Hon, can I get you a different size?" I asked through the curtain.

"No! And don't call me Hon!"

"Yes, Ma'am, I'm sorry, I was trying to be of assist…"

"And don't call me Ma'am!"

Once, a short round woman wanted to be fitted for a long corset with boning reinforcing the seams for her son's wedding. In spite of the measurement, she insisted on trying a smaller size. She successfully squeezed herself in and admired her silhouette in the 3-way mirror. I suggested she walk around and sit down to assure it would be comfortable for the big day. When she sat, the boned ribbing in the corset did its job. The whittled waist and torso did not bend, but all of the extra flesh on her upper body was pushed straight up, sprouting several double chins, and tilting her face back, like a baby bird, drowning. She stood up, and with her hands on her hips, asked for the larger size.

Once, a farmer in his blue denim bib overalls came in to buy his wife a matching lingerie set: panty, slip and bra, for their 25th anniversary. I showed him a beautiful set that was a cocoa color with ivory lace. His callused hands stroked the silky fabric.

"As long as she keeps the tags on, she can return it for a custom fitting," I suggested, "Do you know what size she wears?"

"She's about — your size?"

"OK, lets assume a size 34 slip and band size, and do you know about what cup size she takes for her bra?"

He was cupping his ear toward me. "Yes," he nodded, "She's a little bit of a thing, I would say about cup size ought to do."

I folded the slip and reached for the tissue paper, "Did you want that gift wrapped, Sir?" ∆∆

Who are our bras? If we give them a voice, what do they say?
Here is Jamere Shelby to address that in her poem, I Am Your Bra.

I AM YOUR BRA!
by Jamere Shelby

Full Coverage

Demi-Cup

Push-Up

I AM YOUR BRA!

Cotton

Lace

Silk

I AM YOUR BRA!

White

Black

Nude

I AM YOUR BRA!

Support

Lift

Protect

I AM YOUR BRA! △△

Brava!

Women and power. How do we power through the issues of our breasts and our bras? Times have changed you say. Really? Have they? Let's look. Here is Debra Townsend with her piece, My Place.

MY PLACE
by Debra Townsend

Recently, my son found some old pictures of me when I was in my twenties and thirties. They startled me. I had to admit, reluctantly, that I was quite attractive and successful in those days.

I certainly never felt like it then. In my mind, I was never pretty or good enough. I worked longer hours than anyone else and obsessed over my appearance — dressing for the job I wanted, not the one I had. Every night, I laid out my outfit for the next day, right down to the matching bra and panties, ever mindful of my mother's warning that I could be hit by a bus.

Just after my 30th birthday, I landed a dream job in communications for the state Senate, a chance to use my double major in journalism and political science. I don't recall my official title. It was the '80s and I was usually referred to as the PR gal.

I worked for the majority caucus and its 20 members, writing newsletters, press releases and speeches for all of them. I can still see myself skittering through the Capitol from office to office in my pantsuits and man-tailored blouses, a prized leather portfolio tucked under my arm.

One of the most important senators was the 63-year-old chairman of a major committee who was often referred to as the "Giant of the Senate." A pragmatic farmer representing a rural region, he was widely respected for his down-home wisdom and good-natured humor.

Late one afternoon, I was summoned to his office to work on a press release about an omnibus budget bill to be introduced later that week. I was excited to take on such a high-profile project and looking forward to seeing him. He was always friendly to me in a fatherly way and I was secretly thrilled to be one of his pets. When I arrived, I was waved into his private office by one of the three secretaries out front.

The Senator was on the phone, leaning back in a large maroon recliner. I sat down to wait in a straight-backed chair on the other side of his sprawling oak desk. He hung up and chatted with me politely before turning to the budget bill. It took him an awfully long time to review the details. It was starting to get dark and I heard the secretaries wishing each other good night and departing. Not long after they'd gone, he finished up his instructions. "I'd better walk you out," he said. "The ladies may have locked up."

He strode ahead of me through the main office and into a narrow vestibule leading to the exit. He seemed to be fumbling with the lock. And then, in one fell swoop, he wheeled around and lunged at me, tugging at my blouse and reaching into my bra. I lurched away and backed up against the wall. He slapped both of his big farmer hands on either side of my shoulders and kissed me hard, tongue and all.

I had better knees and reflexes back then. I slid along the wall to the floor, crawled between his legs, threw myself out the door, and ran through the empty halls of the Capitol to my car. I locked all the doors and sat there a few minutes rearranging my blouse, my bra, my thoughts.

Back at my apartment, I took a shower and called my sister who was working in a women's executive program at GM back then. I burbled out what happened. Her advice was calm and business-like. "You must report him." But could I? That night, I barely slept.

The next morning, I arrived at work, bleary-eyed and tardy. As I hustled through the Capitol Rotunda I was chastened to hear the Senate being gaveled into session. It was considered bad form for a lowly staffer to enter the chamber after the powerful had been seated. The Sergeant-at-Arms took pity on me and opened the grand entrance doors a sliver as he shushed and ushered me through.

Praying for invisibility, I tiptoed down the aisle toward the staff anteroom, realizing I would have to pass my attacker. His feet were up on his Senate desk and he was smoking a cigarette. He eyed me intently through the haze.

I cast my own eyes to the ornate carpet beneath my feet. "Good morning, Senator," I whispered.

I knew my place. ΔΔ

And how do you maintain your power under threat of death?
Let's let Sara Weeks lead us through that minefield
with her piece, Boob World.

BOOB WORLD
by Sara Weeks

The party is out on the patio. Carrying a large tray, the cantaloupe rolls over to the edge, the honeydew careens over to the other edge then almost spills over the front. I'm talking about my boobs and trying to contain all that produce in a bra. When you have 42 DDs, life is not a party, it's a party platter.

To add to the festivities, will my front shirt button pop and put someone's eye out?

When speaking to my son's friend over by the bbq, how will I get his eyes to my eye level without ducking my head to meet his and pull them up? (Hello.....up here.)

They weren't always this size. With each kid the produce section grew. After my fourth child, no bra could contain it. (slow look at bras) Imagine two screaming toddlers clinging to your neck who don't want to walk anymore. Imagine those two twelve pound monsters strapped to you, 24/7, bending over to put on your shoes......cleaning out the car. I can't even see the plant I'm trying to re-pot! GAAH......AND!!... My tata's enter a room before I Do.

That's life with 42DDs.

After a while, they came to be life-like, like...twins... but each with its own personality.

At bedtime, lying on my right side, my right boob (or Sister on the Right) would splay out, stretching to the breaking point like she's laying out for a tan. But Sister on the Left feels ignored and has to smother Sister on the Right, so my back and neck strain to keep the peace. The infighting between the girls will subconsciously push me onto my back because my sternum is the referee dragging them apart. Waking up is agony. Each tot having been on their own, pouting in their respective corners, makes sure my skin hurts from being stretched and pulled with them trying to get back together.

Wearing a bra to bed is of no use. (slow look at bras.)

Well maybe...............if it was made of metal.

At my physical in 2013, Dr. Darcy noticed the twins effect on my posture.

"Sara, have you considered breast reduction?"

"I've fantasized about it forever," I said.

"There's a plastic surgeon in your network."

"Darcy, I don't qualify. As big as these babies are, they're several weight grams under the requirement for insurance to pay for it."

"I believe they've expanded the guidelines. Here's the name. Let me know what you find out." The plastic surgeon said a mammogram was required before any more discussion could take place.

Uh-oh. They found something on the right side. Worse, they found four somethings. After christening the tumors, Bush, Cheney, Rumsfeld and Wolfowitz, I chose to remove both breasts. I didn't want the risk of it spreading.

My husband said he didn't care if my breasts were removed. He just wanted me cancer free. I felt I was too young to be breastless and had reconstruction done at the same time as the mastectomies.

What they don't tell you about implants though...................is the way...........they.... FEEL on the inside. The outside looks natural, but imagine a soda can. Now stomp it flat and insert it into your breast skin. Yep, it feels like a clinking, clanking, tin can recycling center in there. Every move you make, large or small, you get pinched and gouged. After three months of torture, I had them removed. No more pain.

With the total loss of hair from chemo, I could've never imagined I'd go into my golden years looking like Curly from the Three Stooges. It took months and months to grow back and finally it did.

As for my overall appearance, I've had to accept the fact I'm left with the body of an over-grown nine-year -old boy.

And…. it's five years later and life is certainly different. A widow now for three years, I've noticed no man under the age of 50 casts a glance my way. The ones over 50 that do look at you, mostly just want you for sex and hey, can you make me a sandwich……… or……..……they gaze at the sturdiness of your legs, looking for a nurse in their old age.

But another aspect of life has changed as well. After decades of the wrong kind of attention because of my chest size, I now have a blissful serenity, no more leering looks and no more……(look at bras)…....bras. ΔΔ

Ownership is power. Or so says writer Leslie Sittner
in her poem, They-Them-Mine.

THEY - THEM - MINE
by Leslie Sittner

They developed fast when I was eleven

They were sore tender unripe apricots without the fuzz

I begged for a training bra

Mom said I was too young

gave me cocoa butter to rub on Them instead

Finally getting the training bra, They felt coddled

They outgrew it in two weeks

Proper bras kept coming as They outgrew the latest cup size

Each time They felt newly contained

Everyone noticed, no one commented

Until high school cheerleading

when They were supported by brutal underwires

that made Them always firm and perky

Boys yelled out "LSMFT"

It did not mean Lucky Strikes Mean Fine Tobacco

Cup-wise, They outgrew available bra sizes

I sewed my own, recycling old underwires

Nursing after childbirth was a goldmine for bras

They were housed in unaccustomed comfort

until nursing ended and the snap flaps had to go

When a man at work told "bodacious ta-ta" jokes

I decided They needed mamoplasty reduction

Arms strapped out wide on a "T" shaped operating table

They were scribed with black marker design lines

With me immobilized but not yet completely asleep

the assisting surgeon laughs,

bellows "They ARE huge, aren't They!"

He jumps when I say "Yes, aren't They…"

Immediately I fall into deep sleep

Recovery is less painful than expected

Bruising and stitches scars are unsightly

but They are five pounds smaller

First day returning to work, They are softly bandaged

but cradled in a new small bra

Brava!

A construction worker in a manhole whistles,

shouts out "Hey, nice size!"

How did he know…?

With caution, eventually I harbored Them

in bras without underwires

I had no idea I could love Them

As a senior, I love Them even more

I now cuddle Them with stretchy, OSFA,

pull-over the head bras

That come in a 3-pack

At last I'm delighted to call Them "Mine" ΔΔ

Brava!

Making decisions about who sees our power is the territory of Alyssa Talanker in her piece, To Strap or Not to Strap.

TO STRAP OR NOT TO STRAP
by Alyssa Talanker

To show one's bra strap in public, or not to show? That is the question. Tis better to live by your mother's rules if over 55, and make sure your bra straps stay hidden in the summer?

Or, tis better to throw out your wireless bra from last year with its stretched out underwires that keep slipping, forcing you into an isolated spot where no one can see you tugging it up?

No other question has so divided generations of female Fashionistas in this century. How did we get to this point?

This battle of the bras started around the year 2000 when young women could be seen walking down the street with bra straps not behaving themselves under tank tops. Ladies in their 70's were silently aghast, doing double takes and muttering to themselves, "Does she really think that's an attractive look?"

For the male species, age was irrelevant as this new look spoke sex whether or not that was the wearer's intention. Besides, did you ever hear an older man tell a younger man wearing his pants below his ass crack, "Get a Belt!"?

Today fair ladies of all ages, I come to bridge the generation gap of brassieres. Allow me to introduce myself. I am well qualified for this undertaking. I was raised in a summer wireless-bra family. Yet, I am a female patriot who supports the bra strap revolution!

To the older naysayers I say, what harm comes from giving bra straps the freedom of expression? Why shouldn't bra straps have the right to be seen wherever they want?

In response you may say, "I'm too old. I can't change the way I think. I know what looks RIGHT when it comes to fashion."

Well, most esteemed Senior Fashionistas, forget what you mothers told you. It's OK to show your bras straps in public when the hot weather arrives. Just think, no longer dost thou need to run to the mall for a new strapless bra when your old strapless underwires give out!

Still not convinced? Then, please indulge me for a few minutes. Close your eyes and imagine yourself one day residing alone in an assisted living facility. The women outnumber the men 10 to 1. Admit it. Don't you want to be the sexy one that catches the eye of that gorgeous man with a full set of gray hair, who works out in the gym and tells hysterical jokes in the communal dining room?

If you answered yes, I offer some French-approved etiquette by Simone Perele of Paris for showing your bra straps in public. Perele is the winner of the 2017 Designer of the Year Award for international lingerie brands. Here are a few fashion tips from Monsieur. (1) Wear straps that are stylish and unfrayed. (2) Make them part of an intentional look. (3) A beautiful bra beneath a lace top can be exquisite.

So there you have it! Senior Fashionistas, don't let the younger ones compare you to George Washington's wife behind your back. 65 is the new 50. Gray hair can be stunning – look at Helen Mirren and Glenn Close – just don't forget to wear makeup.

If you're not planning on going to an assisted living facility anytime soon, then start with the mall. Who knows? You might even find some YOUNGER Fashionista doing a double take and saying to herself, "I'd like to look like THAT when I'm older." ∆∆

Do you want to amp up your power? Look to your elders,
which is what writer Nareen Luz Rivas does in her poem,
My Grandmother at 50.

MY GRANDMOTHER AT 50
by Nareen Luz Rivas

When I was six years old I met my abuela.
This happens when you are the first-born in
a new country. When stories told at the table
are filled with familiar people,
yet you remain outside
a foreigner
never fully grasping
the color blue of their sky
the sea salt taste in their mouths
or the ache they feel for arms outstretched
and soft breath.
"Díselo" my abuela commands me in Spanish,
while headless mannequins mock me

179

with their big bosomed tops
and radio city chorus girl legs.

The salesgirl has already brought her
a dozen brassiers but she says no to all.
"Difficult customer" the young woman's
eyes seem to say, but my abuela
remains unfazed.

"Díselo" says my abuela
and I do not yet understand
the battles she's fought nor
the armor that holds her.
A shield made not of
flimsy gauze and delicate lace,
but melded from strength and courage.

Pounded into grit.
"Díselo" says my abuela.
"Tell her I want to see another one."

Brava!

I hesitate and glance at my abuelo,
discomfit among the chorus girl legs

and I realize

it falls on me to be arms outstretched,
to bridge the gap.
To be her voice.

My abuela. A warrior undeterred.

Neither a country lost nor the long scar
on her breast will conquer her. ΔΔ

Brava!

We've ended each previous year with humor. Not this year.
It just does not feel right. So, let's watch a woman choose a bra under
the most extreme of circumstances and see what it does for her.
Think of her as you take off your bra tonight or choose your armor
tomorrow. Think of her and go out and tell your tale. Here is writer
Pamela Hodges, all the way from Gilbertsville, Pennsylvania,
to read Kilometer 41.

KILOMETER 41
by Pamela Fernuik Hodges

May 22nd, 2018

My room at the Alexander Mackenzie Hotel in Mackenzie, British Columbia, Canada, is on the second floor. As I walk down the hall toward my room, a man in a plaid shirt comes out of his room and walks toward me. I pull the brass key fob into the palm of my hand to hide the engraved room number. I do not make eye contact.

I keep walking, past my room, and step into a recess in the wall. I watch his back until he leaves the floor. When the hallway is empty I go to my room. Once inside, I lock the door and flip the latch. I am alone behind a closed locked door.

May 23rd, 2018

The headboard of my bed in room 216 is on the north wall, in the direction I will drive when I head toward Kilometer 41 on Parsnip Forest Road, a thin black line on the map. I am lying in the direction I need to move. Head first.

I am 2,974 miles from my home in Gilbertsville, Pennsylvania. On the table are boarding passes for the four connecting flights I took from Philadelphia, to Fort Saint John; and the keys to the rental car I drove from Fort Saint John, over the Rocky Mountains to Mackenzie, population 3,507.

The curtains are not pulled completely closed and a band of light tries to enter the darkness of my room. The room smells like salmon from the empty tin in the trash — my supper last night. I hesitate to get out of bed, to put my feet on the floor.

I feel the carpet fibers on my bare feet when I stand up.

In my backpack is a Certified True copy of a Medical Certificate of Death for Karl Hans Schack. Certificate Number 75081411.

Karl Hans Schack, the man my brother and I called Uncle Karl. The man who was not my father's brother; the man who was not my mother's brother. The man who stayed with my family when my father was away on business when I was seven. The man who was given my twin bed with pink covers to sleep in. The man who I was with, in my bedroom, behind a closed door.

I fill the white bathtub. The hot water takes away the anxiety sitting on the surface of my skin.

The clothes I will wear today are laid out like a uniform on my bed. Black socks, black underwear, a long-sleeved black t-shirt, a pair of jeans and two black bras. I don't know what bra to wear when I stand at the marker for Kilometer 41.

One bra is new, a padded underwire bra, with a clasp in the front. The padded cups hold their shape in two separate domes. The other bra is old. It lays flat on the bed. I bought the bra when my daughter was two; she is sixteen now. The bra has six hooks in the back. The second row of hooks are bent from years of hooking and unhooking. There is no padding, no underwire. White elastic on the sides of the bra comes through the fabric in small spirals.

What bra should I wear?

Line item #10 of The Certified true copy of a Medical Certificate of Death for Karl Hans Schack states the manner of death. A lowercase case x is typed in the box next to suicide. Line item #14 asks, in capital letters, HOW DID THE INJURY OCCUR? (describe circumstances.) The answer is typed: Self-inflicted gunshot wound to the head.

Line item #5 states, in capital letters, PLACE OF DEATH. The answer is typed, Kilometer 41, Parsnip Forest Road – near Mackenzie, B.C.

What bra will I wear?

I put on the new padded bra with underwire.

The long sleeves of my black t-shirt cover my recent tattoos. Yes in 60 point bold, Times New Roman on my right forearm. Yes, to not asking for permission.

And the tattoo, no, in 60 Point bold Futura on my left forearm, outlined in a black box: A firm boundary.

No, you can't touch me. No is a complete sentence.

The underwire on the new bra cuts into my skin.

I unhook the front clasp of the padded bra and take it off. I put on the faded black bra with white elastic spiraling out of the fabric. The familiar is comforting.

I open the locked door of room 216 and head north, to Kilometer 41. ΔΔ

And that's it.
At least,
that's it for now.

BraVa! lives on and in doing so, spreads the word that when you buy a bra for yourself that you should also buy one for them — buy a bra for that person in need.
So do so, please, and let us support one another in this fine and meaningful way.

Monetary contributions toward the purchase of bras can be made online at www.ywca-gcr.org/donation, or you can drop off or mail bras year-round to YWCA-GCR at 21 First Street, Troy, NY 12180. For more information on how you can support YWCA-GCR, please contact us at:

EMAIL: info@ywca-gcr.org TELEPHONE: 518-274-7100.

BIOGRAPHIES

Lisa Barone

Lisa Barone is a writer, marketer and strategist with fifteen years in the field helping brands find their voice to create smarter marketing. Outside of work, she's wild about being outdoors, memoir and, most obsessively, her son Henry. **82**

Jillina "J-Bax" Baxter

Jillina "J-Bax" Baxter is the author of two mass-market books of poetry. A former entertainment writer and photographer for various print and on-line publications, she is currently working on publishing her third book of poetry, which is due to be available later this year. **17**

Jill Bryce

Jill Bryce is the author of several stories. A reporter at the Daily Gazette in Schenectady for twenty-five years, and prior to that at the Troy Record, she is working on a book entitled *Sun Spots*, and is a realtor at the family business, Bryce Real Estate in Troy. **155**

Diane Cameron

Diane Cameron is the author of three books. She writes and blogs about personal growth, popular culture and recovery. She is a newspaper columnist, nonprofit consultant, recovery coach and spiritual director. She lives in Albany New York. **20,124**

Kate Cohen

Kate Cohen is a writer and editor. She lives on a farm in Albany with her husband and three children. She wears a size 36C but always wished she were smaller. **79**

D. Colin

D. Colin is a poet and dreamchaser holding degrees in English and Africana Studies. She is the author of *Dreaming in Kreyol* and published in Ink & Nebula. One of NY Capital Region's Creatives under 40 in The Collaborative, she is also a NYS Writers Institute and Cave Canem Fellow. **152**

Susan Comninos

Susan Comninos is a poet and journalist. Her poetry has recently appeared in the Harvard Review Online, Rattle, Subtropics, The Common and North American Review. Her journalism has appeared in The Atlantic Online, The Boston Globe and others. She has completed a debut book manuscript, *Out of Nowhere: poems,* which seeks a publisher. **127**

Brava!

Megan Culhane Galbraith

Megan Culhane Galbraith is a writer and visual artist. Her work was listed as Notable in Best American Essays 2017 and has been nominated for two Pushcart Prizes. Find her in Redivider, Longreads, Hotel Amerika, Catapult, and Monkeybicycle, among others. She is Associate Director of the Bennington Writing Seminars. **53**

Joseph Di Bari

Joseph Di Bari is a retired biology teacher from Troy HS. He grew up in New York City. His first novel, entitled *Beyond Centerfield,* was published in February of 2016. It is a baseball, time travel and sex fantasy. The second book of the series is *Beyond A Masterpiece.* Both are available at Troy Market Block Books, Stuyvesant Plaza Bookhouse and Amazon. **39**

Denise DiNoto

Denise DiNoto works an advocate for all disabled people who strive to live independently. A former Rotary youth exchange student, she speaks at national and international conferences

about how this experience changed her life. She is working on her first memoir, a love story to her five older sisters. **48,92,106,140**

Sandra DiNoto

Sandy DiNoto lives in Trendy Troy. Her professional experience includes a combination of successful ventures in marketing, communications and philanthropy. She currently directs marketing efforts for a local law firm and is an active community volunteer. She is passionate about cookies and blogs about them at cookiebake.wordpresss.com. **68**

Pamela Fernuik Hodges

Pamela Fernuik Hodges is the author of *The Artist's Manifesto: Fight Resistance and Create.* She writes about art, creativity, and thoughts on life at www.pamelahodges.com. She encourages you to believe in yourself and your ability to create. Pamela is currently the typist for her cat, Harper, who blogs at www. thecatwhowrites.com. **74,182**

Missy Frenyea

Missy Frenyea wants to live in a world where it's always October, the internet is free and everything tastes as good as cheese. She's an avid hiker, sports fan and self-proclaimed science geek. When she's not hiking the Appalachian Trail with her partner, Lori, and dog, Bailey, you can find her exploring new breweries searching for the perfect IPA and solving the mysteries of the Universe. Missy has been wearing bras on and off since 1980 and currently lives in the Hudson Valley. **42**

Deirdre Greco

Deirdre Greco is the founder and director of Samaritan-Rensselaer Children's Center, mother of two and grandmother of two. She has taken writing courses at the Arts Center of the Capital Region for several years and enjoys sharing stories from her life with others. **88**

Jennifer Hixon

Jennifer Hixon no longer feels the need to wear her plastron. 114

Opal Ingram

Opal Ingram is an author and poet from New York City. She was raised on the lower east side of New York and currently lives In the Capital Region of New York. She is a short story writer and has self-published six books and six translated books including *Like a Rag Doll, Black Stockings,* and *360 & 361.*She also is a lyrical writer and featured in several literary poetry journals. 91,109,143

Brenda Kilianski

Brenda Kilianski is a playwright, dramaturg and poet living in Albany New York. Her play *Free Radicals* was published by Chicago Dramaworks in 2016. She was awarded an Individual Artist Commission from NYSCA in 2018 to write the play *Beer & Bullets, Billiards & Bells: Manufacturing Albany.* 71

Alice Lichtenstein

Alice Lichtenstein is the author of three novels: *The Genius of the World* (Zoland Books, 2000); *Lost,* (Scribner, 2010); and *the forthcoming, The Crime of Being* (Upper Hand Press, November 2019). Her story, "Revision," (Narrative Magazine) was nominated for a 2019 Pushcart Prize Award. Lichtenstein teaches fiction at Hartwick College in Oneonta New York. 23

Tina Lincer

Tina Lincer is a writer and artist whose essays and articles have been featured in Writer's Digest, The Sun, the New York Daily News, the Albany Times Union and 10 anthologies. She currently works in communications at a private college and exhibits her oil paintings in galleries and other art spaces. **45,129,145**

Nareen Luz Rivas

Nareen Luz Rivas held various roles as a special education teacher in NYC and currently teaches in Guilderland, NY. She holds a B.A. in English Literature from SUNY Oswego and is currently working on her poetry collection. **179**

Patrice Malatestinic

Patrice Malatestinic is a musician, artist/writer who resides in the Capital Region. **29**

Sarah Marquise

Sarah Marquise received her MA in Canadian Literature from McGill University in 2015. She currently resides in Troy and has the pleasure of supporting individuals with developmental disabilities with finding jobs in the community. Poetry continues to be a creative outlet for her, enjoyed best in the company of others. **66**

Christine McCue

Christine McCue is an attorney, writer, public speaker, actor, and comedian. In addition to assisting parents survive the ordeal of family court, she writes a humor blog entitled, My Cape is on Backorder: Supermoms and Other Fairy Tales at http://blog.timesunion.com/mycape **135**

Susan Megna

Susan Megna has moved through the joyful frenzy of family-growing to a meaningful career, and now into a lovely retirement. Her time is spent reading, writing, thinking, talking, listening, laughing, crying, going places, staying home, doing stuff, doing nothing, being with people she loves, being with herself, and sometimes being with a dog. **101**

Dan New

Dan New is a writer of war and military experience. Published in national veteran magazines, and an anthology with the Syracuse Veterans' Writing Group, he has read his work on WAMC and published op/eds in the Albany Times Union. He will facilitate a memoir workshop for the Schenectady Public Library. **116,148**

Ruth Pelham

Ruth Pelham is the founder and executive director of Music Mobile, Inc., a not-for-profit grassroots organization that is now in its 35th year of building peaceful communities through music. Ruth is based in Albany. She performs locally, nationally, and internationally, and has received numerous awards in arts, education, peace, and community building. **35**

Grace Pell

Grace Pell is a published poet. She is currently working on a collection of stories titled *Heartland,* a memoir of repeated transplants: from Kentucky to naval bases during the middle of the last century, from farm to suburb, from military to civilian life. "Confessions from Corsetry" is one excerpt. **158**

Shavina Richardson

Shavina Richardson, a.k.a Blyn Shay, is a creative and outgoing individual who truly loves life. She believes in living hers as if it's her last. She's all about taking chances with no regrets. Shavina is best known as a poet, talent consultant, amateur photographer, writer, manager and the beloved founder of Her Temple Monologues, a performance arts group in Albany, NY as well as the Vice President of United Sisters of New York, a women's empowerment group from Rensselaer, NY. **77, 112**

Marion Roach Smith

Marion Roach Smith is the author of four mass-market books. She owns and runs The Memoir Project, an online lab dedicated to teaching how to write memoir and is the co-founder of BraVa! **51**

Mary Scanlan

Mary Scanlan's essays have been published in both university journals and broadcast on the Capital Region National Public Radio affiliate. Her memoir, *A Will of Her Own,* which recounts her life in the sixties as a young magazine editor who meets and falls in love with a Roman Catholic priest, was published in 2016. **32, 137**

Jamere Shelby

Jamere Shelby is a City of Byram firefighter and GNC Sales Associate. She is a 2018 alumna of the competitive New Leaders Council fellowship for progressive leaders. Miss Shelby founded Yves' Organics, an eco-friendly beverage company that provides healthy juices and smoothies. Her hobbies include competitive amateur boxing and running. **164**

Leslie Sittner

Leslie Sittner's print pieces are available in The Apple Tree by Third Age Press (2016 -17-18), Adirondack Life Magazine, and on public radio. Online poems and prose reside at Silver Birch Press, 101Words, 50 Word Challenge, 50 Word Stories, and Epic Protest Poems. **173**

Alifair Skebe

Alifair Skebe is author of the two poetry books, *El Agua Es la Sangre de la Tierra/water is the blood of the earth,* (written in English), (Finishing Line Press, 2008) and *Love Letters: Les Cartes Postales,* (Basilisk Press, 2004). She is professor of English/Writing in EOP at The University at Albany. **26**

Alyssa Talanker

Alyssa Talanker is an attorney who draws inspiration from those she has helped during her career. Words can give voice to the voiceless, or make an adversary pause and think. Alyssa is an aspiring playwright who blends humor and music into drama. She has written musical comedy to raise money for hunger. As Oscar Wilde said, "Life imitates Art far more than Art imitates Life", so here's to BraVa! 104,176

Debra K. Townsend

Debra K. Townsend is a writer, editor, and communications leader. Her consulting firm, Communications on Demand, has advised and written for nearly 100 organizations, including 50 colleges and universities. She has also served as vice president at Colgate University, Rensselaer Polytechnic Institute, and Skidmore and Bennington Colleges. 166

Carol Tymann

Carol Tymann is a retired kindergarten teacher who enjoys entering writing contests and classes and belongs to a memoir-writing group. She has also acted in some local plays. Carol and her husband spend a lot of time visiting their son, daughter-in-law, and granddaughter in California. 110

Katelynn Ulrich

Katelyn is a poet and performance artist living in Albany. Her work challenges what is commonplace by crafting narratives which personify the mundane. Katelynn uses her craft to disrupt our common acceptance of the world, challenging herself and others to evaluate their perception through poetry. 59

Sara Weeks

Sara Weeks is from East Nassau, NY, and began writing three years ago with Marion Roach Smith. She's appeared in three of the last four BraVas! and considers her participation in the event, her favorite thing to do. She's writing short stories for a book. **95,120,169**

Megan Willis

Megan Willis was a Tang-swilling middle sister raised in the 'burbs outside Detroit who moved to L.A., then Boston, then upstate New York. A copywriter and communications manager, Willis has authored numerous articles and essays exploring such topics as the 1970s, wanderlust, and life with boobs. Willis blogs at www.hornrimproductions.com. **62**

ACKNOWLEDGMENTS

One person listened to this idea, smiled and then said yes. The idea was to raise bras for the women of the Y. The suggested way to do so was to hold one night of memoir readings on the topic of the roles of bras in our lives. That person who said yes is Daquetta Jones, former president of the YWCA-Greater Capital Region. Without her vision -- without that yes -- none of this would be possible.

She said yes and suddenly we had a place to house the first reading and artists to design a logo and stage the set. We had cooks and emcees. We had radio hosts who had us on as guests on their public radio shows; journalists who wrote about the event. There were owners of bra stores who, hearing the pieces on the radio, called and offered their services to fit the bras to the people in need of them and offered to donate bras from their stores.

Brava!

The public responded and bras appeared in the mail, at the front desk at the YWCA-GCR, and at the local businesses who volunteered to take donations.

And then there were the writers. Oh, these stories. We thank every writer for their candor and courage. Some trembled as they read. Some had a friend stand next to them as they told their tales. Everyone had something unique to say.

Thank you to the audiences who, every year, have packed the house.

Our thanks go out to everyone who helped, showed up, sent money, cooked food, designed logos, set up the stage, provided the sound and lights, brought bras, sent bras and laughed, cried and cheered along the way.

Those we can list here are:

Daquetta Jones

Malissa Pilette-McClenon

Marion Roach Smith

Senator Kirsten Gillibrand

Jon Cardinal

The Arts Center of the Capital Region

Pamela Fernuik Hodges

Elizabeth Reiss

Susan Arbetter

Nia Hamm

Tamani Wooley

Elaine Houston

Debra Townsend

Sharon Bates

Paul Miyamoto

Joe Donahue

Bonnie Benson

Shara Branaon-Bender

Brazabra

Corrine Carey

Dali Mamma

Sue Dunkel

Wilhemina Hicks

Colleen Ingerto

Andrea LaRose

Starletta Smith

The Town Shop

Valerie Weaver

Brooklyn Esposito

Jamie Crouse

Michael Ginsberg

Lorna Bailey

Virginia Marinello

Jackie Weaver

Ellen Randolph

Liz Haller

Jennifer Nelson

Lisa Hotte

WE
NEED
YOUR
SUPPORT

DROP OFF A BRA
21 First Street,Troy, NY 12180

MAIL A BRA
21 First Street,Troy, NY 12180

GIVE $ TO BUY BRAS
Monetary contributions toward the purchase of bras
can be made online at www.ywca-gcr.org/donations

QUESTIONS ?
For more information on how you
can support YWCA-GCR,
please contact us!

EMAIL: info@ywca-gcr.org
TELEPHONE: 518-274-7100.

Brava!

Brava!